CONNECTING *the* GENERATIONS

Grandparenting for the New Millennium

Dr. Roma Hanks

Foreword by
CHARLES E. "GUS" WHALEN, JR.
Author, *The Featherbone Principle*

Published through a special grant provided by
Mercantile Stores University and The Warren Featherbone Foundation

FOREWORD

Since midnight last night millions of people have become grandparents for the first time. The number of grandparents in the United States alone is rapidly approaching 96 million. Soon every other person over the age of 35 will be a grandparent. The influence of grandparents and great grandparents on our society will be unlike anything we have ever seen. Connecting the generations in years to come will never be more important.

It's an honor for The Warren Featherbone Foundation to cosponsor with Mercantile Stores University this very special book on grandparenting. Both parent companies, each now well over 100 years old, take a very long view to business and life in general. The new millennium provides our companies with the unique experience of operating in three different centuries.

The Warren Featherbone company was founded in 1883 by an inventor of a product called Featherbone – a stiffener used in women's corsets and sold in department stores like Mercantile's. Our products have become diversified over the years and today we produce Alexis brand infants' wear in the USA for distribution worldwide. One of my good friends reminds me that our company has an unfair business advantage – all of our customers are born naked!

Our paths with you have crossed numerous times over the years because of our connections. We are all connected, directly or indirectly. Though you and I may not know each other we are nevertheless interdependent and part of the greater whole of our society. That connection and our interdependence are the subjects of *The Featherbone Principle, A Declaration of Interdependence*, a book I wrote to describe this phenomenon in a business setting. *Connecting the Generations* by Roma Hanks is a natural progression to perhaps the most powerful of interdependent relationships, that between a grandchild and grandparent.

In many respects our role as parents prepares us for the uniquely important role of grandparents. Grandparents connect the generations. They bring families together in one of life's great second chances, and do so from a different perspective. The grandparent connection, I believe, is spiritually based, which may explain why it is so powerful and why there is almost instant communication at another level and many times without words.

During the time that my and your grandchild will be raised, the projections show that grandparents will be in the majority in our society. That is a comforting thought that points to better days ahead for our society. The emerging grandparent boom will serve to reunite the family of families we call this country.

The grandparenting role is changing and no one understands this better than Dr. Roma Hanks. Dr. Hanks is a professor of sociology and anthropology at the University of South Alabama in Mobile. Well respected and widely published in her field, Roma Hanks is emerging nationally as one who is particularly attuned to the issues and wonderful opportunities facing grandparents and grandchildren. As you will shortly see, Dr. Hanks has a gift for connecting. I believe her work and this book will mark the beginning of a rapidly growing national movement and appreciation for grandparents. That movement will change this country – for the better.

Why is all of this so important? It has been said that "Children are living messages we send to a time we will not see". The best part of our lives as parents and grandparents is in making sure that those messages are connected – and full of hope.

Charles E. (Gus) Whalen, Jr.
President/CEO
The Warren Featherbone Company
Gainesville, Georgia USA

To my parents, Johnnie and E.W.

They left my children Matt and Katie
their strength, their spirit, and their unconditional love.

Some connections are never broken.

INTRODUCTION

Welcome to *Connecting the Generations*. You are about to join a growing alliance of grandparents who want to turn good relationships with their grandchildren into great relationships. Grandparents have an opportunity today that they have never had before. Compared to grandparents in earlier periods, grandparents of the new millennium will be alive and healthy during a larger percentage of their grandchildren's adult lives. Grandparents will not only plant seeds for the future, but they will live to enjoy the benefits of their influence. Families of the 21st century will have proportionally more adults than the families in which we spent our childhood. The connections that you build with your grandchild will have time to blossom and even to be passed to a fourth generation during your lifetime.

Grandparents today are busy. We typically have more connections outside our families than did our parents and grandparents. People in middle life and later may choose to work. Travel, education, fitness, and volunteer activities compete for time that was once devoted to family. I believe this will mean that grandparents will become more concerned about the quality of their grandparenting experiences. Valued time is measured time. If you are going to give up tennis – or perhaps that big job promotion that would require a move to L.A. – to be with your grandchild, then you want to know that your time with him means something special to both of you.

This book is about squeezing the grape. You will learn how to get all that you can out of being who you are, first, and then being the kind of grandparent you have always wanted to be. It may sound selfish, but a successful grandparent is one who takes care of himself or herself first. If you are loved and cared for, you can focus your energy on loving and caring for your grandchild. I want you to be able to get started as soon as possible, so I will keep this introduction short. Here are just a few things to remember as you use this book.

- This book is for you. That's right, this is written for you because I know that you are a living, growing, blossoming person. I wanted you to have a chance to think about how grandparenting changes you and helps you to grow.

- The exercises that you will complete as you move through the chapters in this book are designed with two purposes in mind: to help you explore yourself and to help you get ready for a great relationship with your grandchild. You will explore yourself through reflection, goal setting, planning, and playing. You will get ready to relate to your grandchild by learning some principles of child development and learning how to be his mentor in communicating and relating to others.

- You can use this book at your own pace. The book was designed for use over a full year. Perhaps you have a new grandchild and you want to make his first year special by learning more about yourself and how to relate to him. Someone may have given you this book for Christmas or Hanukkah and you may want to use the new year for this special project. There are twelve chapters. Each chapter has four weeks of activities. You may choose to move faster. The pace is up to you.

- As you begin to use this book, you may consider whether to make it your personal journal or whether you want to share it with your grandchild or her parents, either now or at some later time. If you plan to share the book, you may want to keep handy a small notebook in which to record personal thoughts or memories. After all, you do not want to miss any opportunity to grow; but, you may not want others to know all the thoughts and feelings that this book may inspire. You may share what you learn from the book without actually giving it to someone else.

- After you finish reading *Connecting the Generations* and have completed the exercises, I think you will feel that this book has a special place in your heart and in your memories of your experience as a grandparent. Keep the book where you can refer to it and reflect on the time you have spent growing with your grandchild. You may want to look at this book periodically, especially each year on your grandchild's birthday. It is a reminder of your commitment to be a positive influence in the life of that very special young person. Your grandchild will treasure this keepsake of the unique relationship that you have. This book may even be shared for generations to come.

Time to get started! What you will read in this book is built on several resources: a decade of research that I have done on relationships between the generations; the feelings, fun and frustrations of over 200 grandparents; and the observations of experts in child development, gerontology, psychology, and sociology. Now, it is your turn. You are the expert on your own grandparenting experience. You are the person who knows you best. The journey is yours – Enjoy!

ACKNOWLEDGEMENTS

Connecting the Generations has been a team effort. It began with the vision of Gus Whalen, CEO of The Warren Featherbone Company, who believes that interdependence is our reality and our hope. Thank you, Gus, for that vision and for your support.

Thanks also to so many others who have contributed to this book, to the focus groups and other research efforts that preceded the book, and to our ongoing campaign to recognize grandparents. Thank you to:

- Mike Shannon, President of Gayfers/Maison Blanche, and his colleagues at Mercantile Stores;

- Thomas Rooney, who apparently can work miracles when it comes to organization, planning, and creativity;

- Nell Whalen, an editor who reads with her heart as well as her reference books;

- Phil Bellury, whose creative energy kept the team inspired and on schedule;

- Stan Dark, for illustrations plus;

- Leah Betts, for her patience, talented design, and commitment to the project;

- Dr. Arthur Fisher, whose work and life daily refine the concept of extraordinary consideration;

- Nancy Jones, for significant contributions to sections on child development;

- Maureen Shannon, Daniel Abbott, Annette Moss, Gwen Harper, and Janie Daugherty, for comments on the book draft and support for the project;

- The *Mobile Register*, especially editor Stan Tiner and reporter J. C. Zoghby, for their help in distributing information about the project and research questionnaires;

- Kathryn Smith and Clara Jackson, for fielding untold numbers of phone, fax, and e-mail messages with accuracy and grace;

- Dr. Stephen Thomas and Dr. Paul Pietri for recognizing the potential of my research for helping today's families;

- The more than 200 grandparents who told us their experiences, hopes, joys, and concerns;

- Sam, Abagael, and Sara Evelyn Jones for allowing me to watch up-close their growing connections with their grandparents, their families, and their world.

CHAPTER 1

LOOKING BACK...
LOOKING AHEAD...
LOOKING INSIDE

Matt had stood with his nose pressed against the kitchen window since early morning. Periodically, he would dash off to his room and return with another toy to add to the growing pile near the place where he kept his watch. It was 10:00 a.m. and his grandparents would be arriving any minute. This was about as exciting as life gets for a three-year-old. I walked through the kitchen just as he was turning to go to get another treasure from his room. He looked up at me with the biggest, happiest, most trusting smile I had ever seen on his little boy face.

"Grandpas are for kids, aren't they Mom," he announced, as if he had made a great discovery. And you know what – he had!

Yes, grandparents are for kids...and kids are for grandparents! The relationship between grandparents and grandchildren has at its roots the best interests of the souls of children and adults who may in no other relationship find the love and hope and reason to grow that they find with each other.

Some grandparents may have failed miserably; others may have succeeded wildly in their relationships with spouses, siblings, children, or parents. No matter what other relationships may have brought, suddenly, a new life in the family means a chance to do it all over. This time, you can get it right if it went wrong before or you can repeat an award winning performance in relationships. Grandparents often view grandparenting as a chance to parent again. Whether or not this view of grandparenting is healthy or sound will be discussed later in this book. The point is that grandchildren offer hope. Even the most "hands-off" grandparent can feel the thread of family continuity in the grip of the fingers of a newborn grandchild.

In this chapter, you will learn how to look at yourself, your grandchild, and your family in a way that will help you to see the roles that you and your grandchild have in the history and future of your family. You will read about trends in the American family that may surprise you. In addition, you will see that no matter what is the structure of your own family, you are part of the fabric of American family life. Your beliefs and values matter. Your dreams for your grandchild and your hopes for yourself are not beyond reality – if you know a few important things about direction:

- Who are you? Where are you? How did you get there? Where do you want to be in 5...10...20 years?

- Where do you want your grandchild to be in 5...10...20 years? What will you do to help him get from here to there?

Four activities are provided in this chapter. You may move through the activities at your own pace. If you are using this book as a journal of this year, complete one activity each week this month. It is important to take time to process each activity – to think about what you are doing and to allow yourself to have the memories and feelings that each activity provokes. Remember, you cannot teach your grandchild something that you do not know yourself. Start by completing some exercises that put you in touch with your family history and with your goals for your own life. Then move to some planning exercises for your grandchildren. Finally, think about how you will use your history to create the future that you want for yourself and your grandchild.

Answer the questions to the best of your knowledge. Concentrate on the exercises and read the directions carefully. Get comfortable, relax, and allow at least half an hour of uninterrupted time to complete each exercise on the following pages. Remember that this book is designed to last a year, if you want it to, and each activity is designed to be completed over a week of reflection. That pace will give you time to savor what you are doing and to think about each concept. The result will be a deeper understanding of yourself, your family, and your grandchild.

Time to begin!

WEEK ONE

THE LIVING LOVING FAMILY TREE

A family tree can be more than a visual image of your family. It can be a picture of your memories. If you do more than simply list the names of family members and their relationship to each other, the family tree can come alive with your own childhood! Use this exercise to remember and honor family members in present and past generations. Think about the dynamics of your family relationships, recall important transitions in the family, and remember those relationships that made you feel especially loved as a child.

Look at the "Living Loving Family Tree." Do not write anything at first; rather take the time to remember your family as it was when you were growing up. These are the memories that help you to know yourself, and that self-awareness can be the basis of the kind of soulful relationship with your grandchild that cements the bond of intergenerational love and understanding. Your early family relationships were the context for your own emotional, spiritual, and physical development. Knowing what was important in your own development will help you to identify with your grandchild and to anticipate what he or she may want from relationships during the developmental years of childhood. One of the greatest gifts that you can give your grandchild is a knowledge of your family's heritage. Look into your memory and find your soul – then share with your grandchild the information that is his birthright.

Now, begin to fill in names and relationships on the "Living Loving Family Tree." Give as much information as you like. For example, if Uncle Ted was a great softball player, make a note of that beside his name. Nothing is too unimportant to be shared with your grandchild – not even the fact that your sister's favorite color is purple. Take your time; let the memories flow; and write.

When you finish filling in all the relatives that you can remember, draw a heart around the names of the relatives who made you feel the most loved when you were a child. Now, inside the hearts, write a short sentence or a few words or phrases that describe the attributes or actions that you remember about those people. Draw your memories from your childhood. As an example, my Aunt Stelle always had lemon drop candies for the nieces and nephews who came to visit her. She also had a kind voice and gave lots of loving huggies. If I drew a heart around Aunt Stelle's name on my Living Loving Family Tree, I would write inside that heart, "lemon drops, hugs, and sweet voice."

WEEK TWO

AMERICAN FAMILY QUIZ

How does your family compare with other American families? Are you traditional...normal...alternative...dysfunctional? Take a few minutes to answer some questions about your family and then read some facts that may surprise you about the "traditional" or "typical" American family.

Instructions: Think about the family in which your children spent most of their growing up years. Answer the following questions based on that family.

	Agree	Disagree
1. The number of children in my family is typical for the American family of my time.	_____	_____
2. The work patterns of the adults and teenagers in my family are typical for the American family of my time.	_____	_____
3. There are no more or less divorces in my family than in most other American families of my time.	_____	_____
4. My family has about as much money as the typical family of my time.	_____	_____
5. The values and beliefs held by my family are "mainstream" for families of my time.	_____	_____

Now that you have thought about your family relative to other families of your time, let's look at some historical facts about American families. After you have read the following paragraphs, go back and look at your answers to this quiz and see if you have changed your mind.

WHOSE FAMILY WHEN?

Americans are generally nostalgic about family life. When asked what is the ideal family, we call on periods in our history when we think things were better for children or elders or we think our values were stronger or our beliefs purer. The trouble is,

Americans know very little about the realities of family life throughout our history. For example, we may look back to the turn of the early decades of the 20th century as a time when families were close-knit and parents and children understood the "rules" of family life and lived in homes where there was little conflict, hard work, and clean living. In reality, life was harsher for children of that period than it has been for any generation since. In 1935, one in ten children died before the 15th birthday. My uncle Chester died of pneumonia at the age of three. My grandmother attributed his illness to a cold that he caught attending his father's burial. My grandfather died in his early 40s of influenza. By the time I had pneumonia at the age of one, antibiotics and a week of hospitalization cured my illness. When my son had pneumonia at the age of 7-weeks, we simply visited the family doctor and received appropriate treatment with instructions for managing the illness at home.

How many of us would trade our lifestyles for the idealized homes of the 1940s and 1950s? Probably no one, if we gave much thought to the fact that in 1940 only 1/3 of American homes had running water and about 1/2 had no flush toilets or refrigerators. Education rates were low and poverty rates were high for young people during these times. So why do we think family life was better in the past? Our images of the "American Family" come from media representations such as "The Waltons," "Leave it to Beaver," "Father Knows Best," with some later attempts to represent family life in minority families such as the "The Cosby Show." These glamorized images failed to reflect the realities in American family life. They ignored poverty and single parent families and left us with inaccurate images of the diversity of family life in our time. As the American public watched these idealized families on TV, unrealistic expectations developed that were impossible for many families to fulfill.

Stephanie Coontz's (1992) honest look at the history and development of American family life uncovers realities behind the media myths. Coontz reveals that childhood labor and high infant mortality characterized the period from Victorian times to the Great Depression. She gives good evidence that the idealized family of the 1950s was an anomaly in our history. In fact, the 1950s family which has become the nostalgic standard for many Americans was the product of a ten year period when ages for marriage and parenthood dropped for the first time in over 100 years, birth rates increased, divorce rates declined, and women's education levels fell below those for men. If tradition is based on history, then the family of the 1950s certainly was not the traditional American family.

According to sociologist Beth Rubin of Tulane University, the family in America in the 1990s is a viable and flexible institution. There is considerable variety among families today, with the result that the family we consider to be the "traditional American family" is actually in the minority. At the beginning of the last decade of the 20th century, 42% of all families were married couples with no children, 19% were "step" families, and about 12% were single parent families. One out of two marriages begun today will end in divorce. People are marrying for the first time at later ages than at the middle of this century – now the average age at first marriage is 24 for women and 26 for men. Families are started later as well. Children in their 20s often live with parents. The number of three and four generation households is increasing as life expectancy increases.

Three-fourths of women with school age children and half of women with children under age two are in the workforce. According to sociologist Andrew Cherlin of Johns Hopkins University, the fundamental changes in the American family since the 1950s have been the lessened economic dependence of women on men and the weakening of marriage. These changes may not indicate decline in American family values; rather an increased flexibility in the American family structure and function in response to the demands and opportunities of an increasingly flexible American economy.

What does all of this mean for the family in which your grandchild will grow up? For one thing, the future is less predictable than it may have been for you as a child. Family relationships and work patterns may shift. Communities and organizations outside the family – schools and day care centers – may play important roles in rearing your grandchild. Kinship may be created and dissolved through divorce and remarriage. Family boundaries are more fluid now than they were in our past. Our everyday language includes such terms as "blended families" (children from previous marriages living in a household with their separate parents who are now married to each other) or "chosen families" (children and adults living in the same household but not joined by blood, marriage, or adoption). Today, public institutions may provide funds for living expenses or medical care of the family. You may at some point be cared for by or even share a household with your grandchild. You may have primary responsibility for the care of your grandchild through part of her life. You will probably live to enjoy your great-grandchildren and to participate in their lives as well.

Schools, churches, child care facilities, play groups, and the media provide influences on children that can either enhance or compete with family influences. While there is little evidence that out-of-home care harms children aged two and over, the influences of substitute care on children are not known fully. As children spend more of their lives in public settings, parents and grandparents must be aware that the shared beliefs of their family system may not be held by the people who have the most direct contact with their young family members over most of the day. Child care workers and educators provide essential services for children and their families, but they do not necessarily provide the same socialization influences as parents and grandparents. The next two activities will help you to think about the socializing influences in your life and the goals that you and your family have for your grandchildren.

WEEK THREE

WHO MAKES IT HAPPEN?

Instructions: Think about the influences on your life – when you were a child, a young adult, and today. Answer the following questions as you think about your life as a whole.

	Agree	Disagree
1. I am pretty sure that life will work out the way I want.	_____	_____
2. I usually finish things once I start them.	_____	_____
3. I don't believe in luck – life is what you make it.	_____	_____
4. I like to plan ahead.	_____	_____
5. I usually feel in control of my life and destiny.	_____	_____

Some people feel a sense of internal control. They feel that whatever happens to them is a result of their own thinking, planning, and behaving. Others feel that something outside themselves controls what happens to them. Whether they believe in God or Fate or Nature or Luck, they attribute life's changes to "the powers that be." These people believe in external control. While there is some evidence that an internal sense of control is associated with higher life satisfaction and better performance on some learning tasks, the most important thing for you is to know which orientation is closer to the way you feel about life.

If you agreed with the statements above, your orientation is internal; if you disagreed, your orientation is external. You are likely to feel the same orientation when you think about your grandchild's life. The problem with being oriented toward external control is that it often freezes people; that is it makes them inactive in the face of change or perceived threat. For example, an externally oriented person who loses her job might think, "That's life," and might not actively seek training for a new job. A grandparent who is externally controlled might bemoan a grandchild's drug abuse problem as something that just happened because "that child has always been in trouble and will always be because God is punishing her mother for the bad life she has lived." An internally controlled grandparent might handle the same problem with an aggressive search for information available regarding treatment programs in the grandchild's home town.

If you found by answering these questions that you are externally controlled, you may find it helpful to think about the way that you plan for the future for yourself and your grandchild. There are many positive ways to use external control to your benefit. For example, if you believe that God decides the future, you may also believe in the power of prayer. Psychological as well as spiritual benefits are derived from prayer. Use your prayer time to think about the future and what you would like to have happen and why. Use your time to talk to God as a time to organize your own thinking and responses. If you believe that "Nature takes its course," you may find it helpful to make a chart of all the occurrences that are positive as well as the negatives that Nature sends your way.

WEEK FOUR

GOALS FOR YOURSELF AND YOUR GRANDCHILD

You are at the beginning of a wonderful experience. You have committed to a spiritual relationship with your grandchild. Your first step was made long before you purchased this book. You knew that there was something very special about that little person who came into your life. You felt that only you could teach and guide and love this child in your own special way. Even deeper, in your soul of souls, you knew that there was a shared spirit between you and your grandchild. Somehow that tiny baby or that headstrong toddler was part of you and you were part of her.

Now is the time to plan. Now is the time to think about "who" you always knew you could be and "who" you still want to be. Now is the time to think about "who" you want your grandchild to be – not just the career you want him to pursue, but the person you want him to be. Your grandchild's development can be a catalyst for change in your life as well. Remember that a goal is an outcome that you would like to attain. Take a few moments to think about the goals that you have for yourself and for your grandchild. Complete the exercise suggested here. Write your goals in the spaces provided. For now, just think about the next five years. After you complete this exercise, you may want to list some longer term goals for yourself and your grandchild. Write your goals in the spaces provided. Take time to think about and process what you have written. Then, begin to make it happen!

GOALS FOR MYSELF

GOALS FOR MY GRANDCHILD

THIS YEAR	IN FIVE YEARS	THIS YEAR	IN FIVE YEARS
1._____	1._____	1._____	1._____
_____	_____	_____	_____
_____	_____	_____	_____
2._____	2._____	2._____	2._____
_____	_____	_____	_____
_____	_____	_____	_____
3._____	3._____	3._____	3._____
_____	_____	_____	_____
_____	_____	_____	_____
4._____	4._____	4._____	4._____
_____	_____	_____	_____
_____	_____	_____	_____
5._____	5._____	5._____	5._____
_____	_____	_____	_____
_____	_____	_____	_____

My long-term goals are: _____

_____

_____

_____

_____

_____

_____

GROWTH CHART FOR GRANDPARENTS AND GRANDCHILDREN

As you move through the processes in this book and through this year with your grandchild, come back to this growth chart and record the behaviors that got you closer to the goals that you listed in the previous activity. Refer to this chart as you complete each chapter in this book.

The lives of grandparents and grandchildren are evergreen – always growing...always connected.

Grandparent_____   Grandchild_____

Month 1

Month 2

Month 3

Month 4

Month 5

Month 6

Month 7

Month 8

Month 9

Month 10

Month 11

Month 12

CHAPTER 2

LOVING

How do you know that you are in a loving relationship? Do you feel supported because you are loved? Do the people who say that they love you treat you any better than do your casual acquaintances? "What stupid questions," you may be thinking. "Of course loving causes you to treat a person with honor and to make him feel special." But I am not altogether certain that Americans believe that loving relationships are supportive or that people who love each other necessarily live in harmony. Look at the success of such books as *Women are from Venus and Men are from Mars* – a work based on the assumption that people who are trying to convey love to each other may not even speak the same language when it comes to expressing or interpreting each other's needs. Think about the fact that 1/3 of families have reported physical and/or psychological abuse – an indication that many children grow up wondering why the people who say that they love them treat them with disrespect or violence. "The Women's Movement" and its counter "The Men's Movement" are clear indicators that gender relationships in America are adversarial. Political rhetoric has created a "War Between the Generations," waging a battle over scarce dollars for social welfare programs and medical treatment for the young and the old.

In this chapter, you will examine loving relationships in your life. The principles that you learn will help in relationships between men and women or adults and children. You will learn to take cues from your own spirit. You will discover how to seek out loving relationships that make you feel happy and how to give love in ways that are perceived as loving by those who are important to you. You will learn to create an "us" with the person you love so that you pull together when you face problems or share joys.

Although this non-adversarial approach to loving will improve any close relationship, we will focus on special relationships that you want to improve, including your grandparent/grandchild relationship. Remember that you can teach your grandchild only what you have learned yourself. As you move through the exercises in this chapter, first focus on a loving adult relationship that you want to improve, perhaps a relationship with your spouse or your adult child. Then focus on the relationship that you are building with your grandchild. The exercises in this chapter will help you to learn how real love feels and how to put real love into action.

Let's begin with a definition. ***Love is extraordinary consideration.*** Loving someone is active. Caring may begin with listening sympathetically as someone tells you about the joys or sorrows that have filled his life, but caring becomes loving when you take what you have heard and turn it toward actions that represent how much you want the beloved person's life to be better than it would be if you were not in it. Think about this definition of love for a few moments. It may run counter to your feelings or experiences. Many people concentrate on the pleasant feelings that love brings to them, rather than on the joy that they can give to the people that they love. Think about loving your grandchild. Do you immediately feel the joy of having that wonderful little person in your life or do you think first about all the things that you want to do to make her happy? My guess is that you think first about your own happiness as a grandparent. Don't worry. It is okay to be happy! The trick is to turn all the happiness that you feel into behavior that your grandchild will recognize as love – so let's get started!

There are two simple principles to remember when assessing and improving the loving relationships in your life:

(1) **REAL LOVE FEELS LIKE REAL LOVE.**
(2) **REAL LOVE ACTS LIKE REAL LOVE.**

If you love your grandchild, then thinking of him will make you feel good. Loving your grandchild will also make you do things to show him extraordinary consideration. Sometimes loving him will cause you to discipline him because you care so much about his future success and happiness.

People who love are sensitive to each other – they understand each other's needs and they care enough to listen and to learn how to meet those needs. Absolutely nothing that you and your grandchild say to each other is unimportant. Every word is a clue to help you to find the secret places of the soul. Listen – learn – use the information to grow closer and to be more effective in meeting your grandchild's needs. And for yourself, insist that those who love you listen to you! You deserve consideration and honor. Make yourself heard. Challenge those who say that they love you to prove it with real consideration and esteem. The journey toward loving the special people in your life begins with loving yourself and expecting those who say they love you to demonstrate that love in a way that you can feel.

The first step toward developing extraordinarily considerate close relationships is to learn to use a language of love that is meaningful to you and to the people to whom you want to express love. How do you say "I love you"? What does it take for you to feel that someone loves you? Look around at your close relationships. Have you surrounded yourself with people who are sensitive to you? If you are surrounded by people who are sensitive to you, then you will notice that they treat you with extraordinary consideration. Being with someone that you love should feel noticeably enjoyable and supportive. If you feel alone, unhappy, or afraid to be yourself among people who say that they love you, then you may need to look at the ways in which those people express their love for you and you express your love for them. You may not be speaking love in the same native tongue.

Communication may be difficult even in the closest relationships. People who share a family name do not necessarily share a language of love. Feeling love for a spouse or a child or a grandchild may make us want to understand them and to meet their needs, but loving does not guarantee that our efforts will be successful. Loving can motivate us to learn what causes the person that we love to feel loved, but we must take our loving intentions and turn them into expressions that the beloved person will understand. One problem that Americans have with effective loving is that we overuse the concept of love. This first exercise will help you to find uses of the word "love" that feel appropriate to you so that when you say love – you mean love. Complete the exercise and then take the rest of the week to practice saying what you mean. I love you means *I love you.*

WEEK ONE

"DON'T SAY LOVE UNLESS YOU MEAN IT"

The American lexicon of love is filled with references that imply that love requires no action and no return. Here are some examples of language that suggests that love is a common feeling, that the word "love" has a broad range in emotions that it describes, and that love may be reserved for no one in particular and available even to inanimate objects. This exercise will help you to focus on what love means to you – something you might want to consider before you teach your grandchild about this most important dimension of human emotional experience. Read through all of these sentences without pausing. Then go back and read each one separately. Use the blank under each sentence to rewrite the sentence. In your rewrite, do not use the word "love" unless it is really the most appropriate word in your opinion. Use a dictionary or thesaurus, if you like. Remember, it is okay to use the word "love" in a rewrite of any or all of the sentences, but only if it is the best choice in your opinion.

1. I **love** pepperoni pizza.

    _____

2. Watch him eat. He just **loves** that new brand of dog food.

    _____

3. Kevin seems to **love** math, which is hard for me to believe since his father and I hated it.

    _____

4. I will **love** you forever.

    _____

5. You know, whenever I hear that song, I remember why I **love** it.

    _____

6. I **love** her but sometimes she makes me absolutely furious!

    _____

7. Hey, sweet kitty, do you **love** to be scratched under your chinny-chin-chin?

    _____

8. No one understands why they broke up – they were so in **love**.

    _____

9. Texans **love** barbecue almost as much as they love their mothers.

    _____

10. I **love** you from the bottom of my heart.

    _____

Read your sentences again, paying attention to your feelings. Does love feel different from other emotions? Now you are ready to explore how real love feels to you in the context of a relationship. It is really very simple – real love feels like real love!

WEEK TWO

"Don't Say Love Unless You Act It"
PART ONE -THE LOVING ACTIONS CHART

Now that you have had a week to become familiar with how real love feels, you should be ready to put the feeling into action. This exercise has two parts which will be completed over two weeks. The first part will help you to practice for the second part. If you get the results that I think you will get, then you will want to continue this exercise for the rest of your life. Love in action produces results. The premise is not new here – love as you want to be loved and watch what happens.

Choose a loving relationship that you have with another adult. Choose another relationship that is neutral for you. Use the chart provided here to record actions that you take every day that show your extraordinary consideration for the person that you love and ordinary consideration for the person who is neutral in your life. Remember, if you want someone to feel loved by you, then you must show them that their life is different because you are in it.

Here is an example of the actions that might be recorded:

SAMPLE ACTION CHART	Neutral Person (neighbor...boss...mailperson)	Loved Person (spouse...grandchild...sister)
Sunday	showed courtesy during phone conversation	called to say "I love you" and to thank her for being in my life

Now, you are ready for your own Loving Actions Chart. I hope that you learn a lot about how you turn loving words into actions that show extraordinary consideration – the heart of real love.

LOVING ACTIONS CHART	(Neutral Person)	(Loved Person)
Sunday		
Monday		
Tuesday		
Wednesday		
Thursday		
Friday		
Saturday		

Read your chart. Did you treat the neutral person and the loved person differently? Do you think it was easy for the loved person to know that he was being loved by you? Real love is active.

WEEK THREE

"Don't Say Love Unless You Act It"
Part Two – The Love Book

Now that you have practiced showing extraordinary consideration in order to demonstrate that you really love someone, you can teach your grandchild to do the same. A friend of mine recently talked to me about his son's experience in family therapy. The young family had been saved from divorce when the therapist convinced family members to follow one simple rule: "Treat family members as courteously as you treat strangers and casual acquaintances." Remember the adage, "Familiarity breeds contempt." With intimacy comes the feeling that we know someone so well that we can be ourselves, even if that means behaving badly. How wonderful it is to be able to feel comfortable and accepted. We can say anything and do anything, and those people with whom we are intimate will understand. However, sometimes problems develop when family members forget to honor those with whom they share the most intimate relationships. The wise therapist who worked with my friend's son had simply listened to the family's communication and observed that when they spoke to each other they used language that might be considered rude or inconsiderate in ordinary conversation with non-family members. Once the family realized that they were not treating those whom they said they loved as well as they treated strangers and casual acquaintances, they were able to see how arguments escalated and loving feelings went unnoticed. Courtesy and consideration kept the family intact.

Remember that real love feels like real love and that real love acts like real love. If your grandchild wants you to know that he or she loves you, then you must teach that young person to express love in language that you understand as loving. This exercise will help you to teach your language of love to your grandchild. Think of yourself as an author or book editor who is producing a thesaurus filled with words and phrases that mean love. Illustrate each entry with an action that shows extraordinary consideration. Help your grandchild to be considerate of you. Teach her communication skills so she may be effective in showing you her love throughout your life together.

As you talk to your grandchild about love, use your own terms for loving acts. Intimacy involves building a language that is not shared with the outside world. You and your grandchild will become part of a loving club. You may not have a secret handshake or a decoder ring, but you will have words and looks and feelings that are yours alone to share. Use the space provided on the following page to start your own Love Book to share with your grandchild.

Write in the first column actions that you associate with love. Two have been given to get you started. Then, use your own words to describe each loving action. Use words that you want your grandchild to learn. Next, give your own definition for each loving action. Finally, describe how each action makes you feel. (See the first line as an example.)

THE LOVE BOOK

ACTION	YOUR WORDS	YOUR DEFINITION	YOUR FEELINGS
Hug	Huggies Bear Hug	wrapping arms around each other	warm safe
_____	_____	_____	_____
_____			
Kiss			
_____	_____	_____	_____
_____	_____	_____	_____
_____	_____	_____	_____
_____	_____	_____	_____
_____	_____	_____	_____
_____	_____	_____	_____
_____	_____	_____	_____
_____	_____	_____	_____
_____	_____	_____	_____
_____	_____	_____	_____
_____	_____	_____	_____
_____	_____	_____	_____
_____	_____	_____	_____
_____	_____	_____	_____

WEEK FOUR

"Us"

Building an "us" with your grandchild means getting inside her or his world so that you can share feelings. Eventually, you will have your own language. You will develop secret code words and actions that make both of you laugh and feel that you are the only ones in the world who get the joke. It is up to you to initiate that secret language – your grandchild is busy learning everything there is to know about this world. You must make a place for this relationship, in your own life and in your grandchild's.

Children respond well to repetition and continuity. Tell your grandchild that you are important to her. Say that often. Use the same words and actions to show your importance in his life. This exercise can be used with a very young grandchild or with one who is older. The important elements of the activity are:

- *clarity*
- *significance*
- *repetition and*
- *continuity*

Use the space provided here to write the elements that you will use to build an "us" with your grandchild. Each time you write a letter, have a phone conversation, or see your grandchild, use these words and these actions. If you use them over and over, they will become the "secret handshake" of your relationship with your grandchild. Long after you are gone from his life, these words and actions will bring memories of the person who taught him that love was constant, unconditional, and real.

My special name for my grandchild is _____

The special name that I want my grandchild to call me is _____

_____

_____

I will begin each contact with my grandchild by saying _____

_____

_____

I will close each contact with my grandchild by saying _____

_____

_____

Each time I am with my grandchild I will do this _____

_____

_____

How simple this sounds, but such simple words and acts weave the fabric of "forever." Be close. Be happy. Be "us" with your grandchild. Build your relationship as you want it to be.

REFLECTIONS

CHAPTER 3

LET'S PRETEND

On Sunday morning, when he stands before his congregation in clerical robes and presents his articulate message in a booming voice that fills the church, it is difficult to imagine Phil as the grandfather who drank tea from a tiny cup and nibbled "pretend" ham and butter sandwiches at a tea party with his granddaughters on Saturday afternoon. Yesterday, Phil was in a different world – his grandchildren's world – where he was privileged to be accepted in a ritual part of growing up. Yesterday, Phil played with his granddaughters.

Play is the work of childhood. Through play, children practice their skills in thinking. They try out approaches to building and sustaining relationships. Play provides a context for language development and gives children a useful setting in which to learn to cope with life's problems. In fact, play is so important in a child's coping and adjustment that therapists use play to treat children who have suffered trauma and are having trouble understanding or expressing their feelings. Play is the safe place where children can satisfy the desire to explore.

Styles of play vary by age. Older children are more likely to be concerned about the associations with others who join them in a play situation, while very young children spend more time in solitary play. If you have an infant grandchild, you may have observed him spending long periods just watching his own hands or feet or looking at a mobile as it swings above his crib. Your 4-5 year old grandchild is much more likely to ask you to join in her play activities. Sometimes children engage in "parallel play" with their parents or grandparents, often with the adults not really knowing what is happening. Have you ever scolded a toddler for pulling all the pots and pans out of your kitchen cabinet while you were making dinner? It is likely that the child interpreted that entirely differently than did you. You saw what happened as disruptive and annoying. Your child or grandchild saw it as playing with toys just like the ones with which you were "playing". To the child this was *parallel play*. Including a child in an adult task can be *associative play* for the child. Your grandchild makes little distinction between helping you to "play" in the kitchen making dinner and having you "play" with a kitchen set in her room. In either setting, the child is learning from your interdependent worlds.

Adults are more likely to label as "play" another form of games that we call *cooperative play*. Games, competition aimed at winning, and doing things together such as shopping or going to an amusement park all are forms of cooperative play. Cooperative play helps your grandchild with relationships, especially when there is a group involved in the play activity. This kind of play is more characteristic of middle childhood than of early childhood. Each category of childhood play has its purpose in the development of the child.

As a grandparent, you may wonder how to select games and toys that will be appropriate for the developmental stage of your grandchild. Knowing a few simple principles of child development will make these choices easier and will help you to be successful in your attempts to be accepted in your grandchild's world of play. Remember Phil, the tea-sipping grandfather? Phil was successful in playing with his grandchildren because he followed their lead. He accepted their invitation into their world rather than pulling them into his. A tea party is associative play. The most important aspect of the game is just to be together. Phil's granddaughters were developmentally ready for associative play and he was wise enough to recognize their need simply to be with him and to try on some more adult roles in a safe setting. Here is some information that will help you to be as successful as Phil in responding to your grandchild's need for play.

The National Association for the Education of Young Children (NAEYC) and the National Association of Early Childhood Specialists in State Departments of Education jointly developed some guidelines for developing positive learning situations for children. Although these guidelines are primarily for teachers in day care and preschool settings, I think that some of the principles are worth noting here. Grandparents who want to use play situations as an educational experience for their grandchildren should be aware of these principles:

- The situation should promote interactive learning and encourage the child to construct knowledge.

- The situation should encourage the child to develop positive attitudes about learning.

- The situation should be relevant to the child's life.

- Expectations for the child should be realistic.

- The situation should foster the child's exploration and inquiry rather than focusing on a right or wrong solution.

- The situation should promote feelings of safety, security, and belonging.

- The situation should promote feelings of success, competence, and enjoyment of learning.

- The situation should permit flexibility for children and adults.

Many grandparents have told me that they worry about whether or not they will be on target for their grandchild's developmental level when they play with their grandchildren or use play as an educational tool. The table presented here provides a summary of the stages of social development of a child from birth to 3 years of age. Later in this chapter, another table will provide developmentally appropriate play activities for the first year of your grandchild's life. Although there is much more to learn about child development than can be presented in these brief tables, you can refer to this material for guidelines in playing with or teaching your grandchild. The information in these tables was compiled by child development specialist Nancy Jones, a Validator for the National Academy of Early Childhood Programs.

OVERVIEW OF GROWTH AND DEVELOPMENT BY AGE

AGE	PHYSICAL	EMOTIONAL	SOCIAL
4 weeks	Startle response; Sucking reflex; Grasp reflex; Looks at dangling objects	Gratified by sucking; Responds to mother's emotional attitude; Cries from discomfort	Smiles at 6 weeks; Expresses demands by crying; Responds to being held, fed, changed
3 months	Holds up head; Tries to reach; Focuses actively; Grasps objects	Smiles freely; Shows pleasure and anger; Responds to sound, sight, touch; Recognizes mother	Coos, babbles, gurgles; Laughs aloud; Frolics when played with; Not selective
7 months	Sits in high chair; Manipulates objects; Hand to mouth and visual exploration; Reaches accurately; Turns completely over	Shows affection for all people; Fears loud noises and falling; Shows pleasure, anger, fear and affection	Imitates simple acts; Cries for people; Responds to name; Uses attention getting behavior; Uses syllables – ba, da, ka
10 months	Rolls over and sits up; Stands with support; Creeps or crawls; Bangs and drops objects	Gives affection only with familiar people; Responds to words like "Where's daddy?"	Wants to be with people; Learns by imitation; Waves "bye-bye" and shakes head "no"
15 months	Walks; Finger feeds self; Hands objects to people; Stacks blocks; Scribbles with crayon	Shows sympathy, jealousy, anxiety; Begins positive signs of independence; Some sense of personal identity	Kisses pictures; Asks by pointing; Wants an audience; Begins to imitate domestic duties
18 months	Can walk backwards; Pushes, pulls, bangs, tugs, lugs, plays ball and paints; Cleans up messes	Temper tantrums; Destructive; Distinguishes between "you and me"	Cannot project to future; Puts words together; Plays games alone and with others; Sways to music
2 years	Can kick a ball; Pinches, pushes, kicks, bites; Can copy a circle; Can put on shoes, socks, pants	Negative - exercising control; Ritualistic and self-centered; Fussy eater; Can evidence guilt and show great affection	300 word vocabulary; Can't share; Solitary parallel play; More responsive to hugs or distraction than to discipline; Vacillates between dependence and independence
2-1/2 years	Jumps on both feet; Tiptoes; Builds towers and bridges with blocks; Bladder and bowel control	Goes to extremes; Tries to do both things when given choices; Cannot be forced	Tantrums at peak; Ritualistic; Dawdles when cannot make a choice; 1000 word vocabulary
3 years	Can count but not understand math; Dresses and undresses self; Draws a man on request; Knows some nursery rhymes	Can make simple choices and show self control; Tries to please and conform; Enjoys praise; Frustrated with obstacles	Begins to "wait his turn"; Distinguishes boys and girls; Interest in own body; Loves to be with other children; Highly imaginative

Here are some developmentally appropriate play activities for a very young child. Remember, you may have to redefine "play" for yourself. An infant does not play competitively or cooperatively. For an infant, play is practice in learning the sights and sounds of his world, coordinating the movements of his own body, and interacting with those who are close to him. After you read the activities suggested in this table, think about the games that you played with your children. You may have favorite family games that you will remember. Use those familiar games when they are appropriate for the age and developmental level of your grandchild. Most of all, have fun!

DEVELOPMENTALLY APPROPRIATE PLAY FOR BABY'S FIRST YEAR

Strengthening and Coordinating Movement (0-3 months)
Place the baby on her tummy on a covered surface. Choose a colorful toy and then lie flat facing the baby. Move the toy from side to side so the baby must raise and move her head in order to see it. Use voice disguises to maintain interest. As the baby gets older, she will reach for the toy and move her body in order to get to it.

Strengthening Neck, Arms, and Shoulder Muscles (3-6 months)
Lie back with your head firmly supported by a rolled pillow. Place the baby on your chest. Hold the baby with both of your hands under his arms, around the rib cage. Lift the baby off your chest and into the air then lower him back to your body and let him touch your face. He will stiffen his body and the muscles will be strengthened. Avoid throwing the baby into the air above your head as sudden movements are frightening.

Rolling (3-6 months)
Place the baby on the floor or on the bed over a rolled pillow. Make sure that her arms are free. Hold her around the hips and gently roll her backward and forward. As the baby moves, leg and arm muscles will be strengthened. Eventually, she will use her hands and feet to push and stop. You may get a bonus of cute sounds and smiles as well.

Where Is The Toy? (6-9 months)
Place the baby on the floor on a quilt or pad. Get his attention by saying "Look Brad, here is a ball. It is red and blue." When he notices the ball, place it under a towel. Watch and see if he pulls the towel away to find the ball. If the baby has achieved the concept of object permanence, he will look for the ball. Play this game often and with different objects. It is fun to watch your grandchild gain new concepts and apply them to play situations.

Taking Out The Toy (6-9 months)
Sitting on the floor in front of your grandchild, place a container with toys inside (no lid) in front of the baby. Shake the container to call her attention to the toys. Show her how to take out the toys and put them back into the container, and encourage her to do the same. When she has mastered the task, put a lid on the container. She will enjoy removing the lid to look for the toys. You can add language stimulation by talking about each toy as she discovers it.

Removing and Placing Objects In A Container (9-12 months)
Put a few objects (blocks, clothesline, large plastic snap-together beads) in a large plastic bowl, a paper bag, or a small box. With the baby sitting opposite you, shake the container to get his attention. Dump the objects out and say, "Let's put them back." Place one object back into the container and encourage the baby to do the same. Praise her efforts. When all objects are back in the container, encourage the baby to dump them and start again.

Follow The Leader (9-12 months)
Select several pairs of items, one for you and one for the baby. Sit facing the baby. One at a time take your object from the pair and do something with it – put a cap on your head or throw a scarf in the air. Ask the baby to do the same with his similar object. You can also play this game without objects. Ask the baby to repeat your actions such as patting your head.

Note that ordinary, easy to find materials can be used to play with your grandchild. There is no need to invest in expensive educational toys unless you want to provide some special treat for your grandchild. Here is a list of simple household items that can be used for safe and effective play with an infant or toddler.

- Cardboard boxes of different sizes
- Pots and pans
- Spoons and spatulas
- Smooth wooden blocks
- Bells (supervise play with these as the clapper can be pulled off and swallowed)
- Unbreakable mirrors
- Nesting jars, cans, or boxes
- Colorful paper or posters

There are other sources of information in your community that will help you to choose toys and play activities that are appropriate for your grandchild's particular stage of development. If you are interested in learning more about child development, contact your local chapter of the National Association for the Education of Young Children. The national office of NAEYC can give you information about the local chapter. You can reach the staff of NAEYC at 1-800-424-2460. Another source of information about child development is your County Extension Agent. For your local agent's address and phone number, contact your state's Cooperative Extension Service, listed in the blue pages of your telephone directory. If there is a community college or university in your area, you may be able to find information through the departments of Psychology, Education, Child Development, or Human Ecology. Check the directory at your local institution of higher education. Of course, local bookstores, public libraries, and the internet are also sources of information about child development and choosing appropriate games and toys. Try these internet resources for information on developmentally appropriate toys, games, and books:

- http://place.scholastic.com/ect/index.htm
  Tips for educational toys and activities

- http://www.family.com/
  Disney's guide to toys and activities

- http://www.parentsplace.com/index.html
  Advice for parents and other adults

- http://www.naeyc.org/naeyc/resource.htm
  Advice for parents, teachers, grandparents and anyone who works with children

- http://www.pathfinder.com/ParentTime/Welcome/
  Advice on toys and many child development issues, customized by age

Now, let's try some activities that get you ready to enjoy playing with your grandchild. Remember, you and your grandchild are growing together, so we will start with YOU.

WEEK ONE

YOUR INNER CHILD AND HOW IT PLAYS

This chapter so far has focused on your grandchild's development and age appropriate play. I would like to pause for a moment and ask you to think about what play means to you. What do you enjoy doing? What makes you feel free and childlike? When do you feel gleeful and happy? Do you like to play team sports or take to the tennis courts for one-on-one competition? Do you enjoy creative activities such as painting, playing music, or doing crafts? Does your play involve being out of doors or are you a couch potato or card player who would rather stay inside your home with family or friends? Whatever you do for recreation, you are probably tapping into your childhood when you play as an adult.

Too often, the child within us is ignored. We have misinterpreted the theories of Freud, Erikson, Piaget and other developmentalists. Yes, the developing human does go through stages and it is important that at each stage the developing individual resolves issues and grows into the next level of independence and self-awareness. However, in order to grow as a human being, you do not need to forget what it was like to be a child or to turn your back on the wonders of childhood. Think about this example. John is a 30-year-old construction worker. He loves turkey sandwiches and has since his grandmother made the first and best one that he remembers, but he hates mayonnaise. Whenever John orders a turkey sandwich from the deli, he asks for "no mayo." Whenever John's sandwich comes back with mayo, he has a temper tantrum. John never politely asks the server to get another sandwich. Instead he raves about the stupidity of the deli's staff and the state of a world in which people cannot understand a simple direction like "no mayo." No harm is likely to come from John's bringing his fond childhood memories of his grandmother's turkey sandwiches into his adult life. However, John may someday run into trouble if he continues to react with childish temper tantrums when his lunch order comes out wrong. Adults need to stay in touch with the memories and feelings of childhood, but they need to manage the current world with adult skills. Freud, Erikson, Piaget and others whose observations about human behavior emphasized a developmental sequence never meant to encourage adults to reject the heart and soul of the child within in the process of learning to cope with growth and development.

Psychotherapist Carl Jung called the natural child that is inside all of us the "wonder child." Building on Jung's work, present day popular author and therapist

John Bradshaw has emphasized the healing potential of tapping the exploration, creativity, and awe that our "inner child" offers each of us every day. I believe that the most effective grandparents are those who have not forgotten their own feelings as children. I believe that you are your best in your relationship with your grandchild when you reach into your memories and pull out, not only *what you did* as a child, but *how it felt* to do it.

This first exercise is designed to help you to find your inner child and to use that wonderful part of yourself to help you relate to your grandchild through play. What a marvelous experience to be able to feel those long-forgotten feelings of wonder as you rediscover play and at the same time watch your grandchild explore the world through playing with you. 1-2-3...ready...go!

Answer a few simple questions about yourself. As you answer these questions, try to remember your feelings as a child. Allow yourself to feel the awe of exploring something new or taking risks. Giggle, scream, hide your eyes, make the gestures and sounds that you made when you were playing your childhood games. Find your inner child who still thinks life is fun and wonderful.

QUESTIONS ABOUT YOUR INNER CHILD AND HOW HE PLAYS:

1. Describe the first "game" you can remember playing as a child. _____

    _____

    _____

    _____

2. When you were a child, did you prefer playing alone or with other children? Why?

    _____

    _____

    _____

3. What was your favorite childhood game? Why? _____

    _____

    _____

    _____

4. What game did you dislike most as a child? Why? _____

    _____

    _____

    _____

5. What game from your childhood would you most like to play with your grandchild? Why? _____

    _____

    _____

    _____

6. What do you do now as an adult that gives you the same feelings as those that you remember from playing your favorite childhood game?

    _____

    _____

    _____

WEEK TWO

YOUR TURN TO PLAY

The best gift that you can give your grandchild is a healthy, happy grandparent. Before you can love and care for your grandchild, you need to love and care for yourself. This may sound selfish, but remember, it takes more emotional and physical energy to feel sorry for a neglected you than it does to take care of you from the start! This exercise will help you to take care of yourself and to get ready to play with your grandchild. Now that you know what your inner child enjoys – now that you have been in touch with the child inside yourself – it is time to take some action. Give that inner child the power to lead the adult you on a wonderful journey of discovery. Start something new that is just for you. Once you are on your own path of adventure and discovery, you can turn your attention to the wonderfully exciting world of discovery that waits in your relationship with your grandchild.

1. What is one thing that you have always wanted to do for fun, but never tried?

_____

_____

_____

_____

_____

2. NO EXCUSES! Go to your phone book, computer, or other source of information and do not stop looking until you have successfully determined the best local source for getting you started with the activity that you described in your answer to question #1. Write here all the information that you need to get started.

Phone numbers: _____

_____

_____

Educational/ licensing requirements: _____

_____

_____

Timetable for starting: _____

_____

_____

3. Make a phone call or visit to the appropriate place to get started doing the activity that you described in your response to question #1. Write here the results of your inquiry and the date and time when you will start doing what you really want to do. It's your turn!

I found out that _____

_____

_____

I will start on _____

_____

_____

Have Fun!!!

WEEK THREE

INTRODUCING YOUR INNER CHILD TO YOUR GRANDCHILD

Now that you have found your inner child and you have given yourself permission to do something fun – just for yourself – you are ready to play with your grandchild. Connecting the generations means finding that part of yourself that can relate to those who are younger than you. You can connect with your grandchild if you forget about your outsides and reach into your insides and let go that wonderful childlike spirit that wants to explore, to learn, and to play.

Turn back a few pages to the tables that present age appropriate play activities for your grandchild. Select one or two activities that you think will be fun for your grandchild and for you. Play with your grandchild for at least half an hour. As you play, think about your feelings. Allow your inner child to play along with you. Try to imagine the "wonder child" inside you playing with your grandchild. Imagine how your inner child feels. Imagine how your grandchild feels. When you finish your play session, write your feelings here. Take time to reflect and to enjoy those feelings. You just made a connection between your inner child and your grandchild. You just made a connection that your soul will never forget.

When I play with my grandchild, my inner child feels _____

_____

_____

_____

_____

When I play with my grandchild, I think my grandchild feels _____

_____

_____

_____

_____

This is fun! The next time I play with my grandchild, I want to feel _____

_____

_____

_____

_____

The next time I play with my grandchild, I want her (him) to feel _____

_____

_____

_____

_____

WEEK FOUR

WHAT ARE YOU DOING IN MY SANDBOX?

As your grandchild grows, her attitudes about playing will change. When she is young, she will eagerly play with familiar adults. You will enjoy seeing her face light up because she recognizes you. Eventually, play will become a way to try out independent roles. She may want to create a world apart from yours where she can be alone or with friends her own age. She will notice that you are an adult and she is a child and she may find your presence in her world of play to be embarrassing or annoying. How will you handle this "rejection"?

The most important thing for you to do is to be flexible as your grandchild grows. Remember, when he shows you his independence, he is showing you that the growth process is going successfully. As difficult as it may be to let go, the successful parent or grandparent is teaching the child eventually to get along without adult supervision. Play is a safe way for your grandchild to practice his own decision making and relationship skills. After all, the process has happened to you. Think back across your life. It was okay when your mom or dad sat on your patio or front porch and watched you play tag with the little kid from across the street. My guess is that you "just about died" when your parents insisted on making prom pictures and that nobody invited your parents when you went off to play on that honeymoon to Hawaii.

This is a good time to stop and to think about your own feelings about your grandchild as they relate both to his play and to his role in your life. What need is filled in your life when you play with your grandchild? Are you recapturing the childhood that you never had? Are you using child's play with your grandchild to compensate for a lack of fun in your own life? Are you having fun *through* your grandchild, rather than *with* him? Are you trying to amend your parenting by playing with your grandchild as you never had the time or energy to play with your child? Think about your needs for fun that are independent of your grandchild. Think about his needs for play that are independent of you. Use the space below to write your thoughts about the role of play in your life and in the life of your grandchild. Some reflection now will help you to avoid pain when your grandchild exerts his independence later.

Reflections on Play: _____

_____

_____

_____

_____

_____

_____

_____

_____

_____

_____

_____

_____

_____

CHAPTER 4

BUILDING SPIRITUAL CONNECTIONS IN RELATIONSHIPS:

THE SOULFUL GRANDPARENT

"We're lukewarm people for all our feast days and hard work. Not much touches us, but we long to be touched...Our children frighten us in their intimacy, but we make sure they grow up like us. Lukewarm like us."

— Jeannette Winterson, *The Passion*, 1989

This chapter is about connections. Attachments begin in that deep place within yourself where you keep the treasures of your heart. Some people keep that place locked away and rarely explore it themselves or with anyone else. Others reach into that place every time they smile or touch or share a thought. Connections are grounded in that place in your heart. Some call it the soul. Whatever name you give it, remember that you have within yourself a place of connection. Some find that religion or love or creative expression are the keys to unlock the carefully kept treasures of the soul. In this chapter, you will find ways to explore your feelings, methods for looking into your depths and for sharing what you find there with those who are close to you. Your ability to share the spiritual part of yourself with your grandchild begins with finding it for yourself.

The process of this book assumes that you are committed to developing relationships that have meaning, depth, and passion. You look around and see lukewarm relationships – people who relate in words but miss each other's souls – and you wonder why. You want more than a lukewarm relationship with your grandchild. You want your grandchild to run to you and give you the biggest, warmest, most soulful hugs possible. As your grandchild grows, you want her or him to be able to tell you the most intimate thoughts, wildest dreams, and deepest commitments. Religion, politics, romance, personal decisions, physical changes – you would like nothing to be off-limits in your conversations with your grandchild. You have reached a time in your own developmental process when you are not afraid. You want to know why people say or do the things that you observe. You like honesty and you crave intimacy in friendships and family relationships.

Am I right so far? I hope that I am because I want to believe that we are a caring generation and that we are raising our children and grandchildren as a generation of *vertical people*, aware of themselves from the inside out and able to draw from their depths in relating to others. I am confident that soulful grandparenting is the key to raising a soulful and caring generation. The time is perfect for you to be the teacher of your grandchild's soul. If you and your grandchild can connect – soul to soul, spirit to spirit, heart to heart – then you can save her from the lukewarm life. You can give him the passion to feel real love, real joy, real commitment, real faith.

WEEK ONE

VERTICAL AND HORIZONTAL CONNECTIONS: "GRANDPA OAK AND GRANDMA IVY"

Let's begin a process of discovery, or for some of you, a process of renewal. Think about two very different plants that may be growing in your yard or in the park nearby. An oak tree has a deep taproot that holds it firmly in the ground and nourishes it from a central source. Oh yes, the oak tree has other roots as well that reach in many directions to help steady the plant against a storm and give it more nourishment, but the taproot is its anchor. The ivy that climbs up your garden wall has much shallower roots than the oak tree. The ivy spreads those roots in many directions and puts down new roots wherever it goes. People have different kinds of roots as well. Some people are nourished by a few deep friendships that may have begun when they were very young and continue throughout life. Others make new friends easily and count their friendships in numbers of people rather than length of time. They enjoy different people for different activities.

Your preferences may change as you move through life, but you probably have a style of being you that has been yours since you were a child. If you take the time to get in touch with your groundings – that part of you that is deep in your soul – you will discover that most of your relationships follow a pattern. They are either intimate or they are casual. You build relationships either by empathizing and looking into the other person's soul and allowing him or her to look into yours or you prefer to get to know "things" about the other person and then to share casual experiences as your friendship grows. You keep your friendships over many years or you move along to new friends as your life changes. You may use both styles of relating, the choice depending on the person and the situation. Your style follows you into your roles as parent and grandparent. As your relationship with your grandchild develops, you will find that you either go for a deep spiritual relationship with him, sharing confidences and helping him to solve problems, or you have great interest in his activities and accomplishments but little knowledge of what goes on inside. The difference in the way that you relate comes from the two faces of you. Grandpa Oak is your vertical self. It is grounded in your own history, the principles in which you believe, and the family values that have made you who you are. Grandpa Oak lives in your soul. Your Grandma Ivy is your horizontal self. It is more superficial, more concerned with the fun and drama of everyday life and everyday relationships.

Let's think for a moment about how you select a gift for your grandchild's birthday. When you are in your Grandpa Oak mode, you may carefully research gift possibilities, looking for something that has meaning, educational value, or is linked to your family in a special way. A gift that comes from this vertical self might be a toy that you enjoyed as a child or the first book that you ever read, while a gift from your horizontal self might be a toy that your neighbor said her grandchild enjoyed. Both gifts are thoughtful and loving, but one draws from the groundings of your soul and the other could come from anyone. Remember, if you and your grandchild are to have an extraordinary relationship, **you** will have to begin the process by treating your grandchild in an extraordinary way. If you are a grounded, or vertical, grandparent – Grandpa Oak – you will understand that the relationship you have with your grandchild is grounded in your soul. There is no better way to show that precious young person that you want to build a uniquely connected relationship with him than to share part of yourself whenever you play, celebrate, or even when you say "no."

Use this exercise and those that follow in this chapter to go deeper and deeper to find that place where your soulful relationships are grounded. You will practice with these exercises and you will learn to teach your grandchild to connect with what is deep inside him – his vertical self. Then, you and your grandchild can create a grounded bond, a connection that will never be broken.

How would you describe your "Grandma Ivy" horizontal self?

No, your horizontal self is not the you who falls asleep on the sofa halfway through a conversation with your spouse. Your horizontal self is your superficially connected self. When most of us are asked to describe ourselves, we answer that question with some facts about our height, weight, hair color, job title, marital status, or other facts about our appearance, interests, or relationships. These are descriptors of our *horizontal selves*. They represent our image of ourselves in relation to other people and our external connections to our social world. Imagine yourself standing with your arms stretched widely from your sides. Think about touching the people with whom you live, work, or go to church. Anyone that you can touch with your outstretched arms is part of your horizontal community. We shake hands to signify acceptance of people as part of our horizontal communities. We hug our relatives and special friends to bring them into our horizontal space. Sometimes we extend our horizontal boundaries by writing letters, making phone calls, or getting online with our computers. Still, our horizontal relationships are rather superficially connected – to the outside of ourselves.

In order to imagine your horizontal self, it may help to imagine that you are playing "Ring Around the Roses" in a huge circle with all the people who help you to define your horizontal self. Later, when you want to teach your grandchild the difference between horizontal and vertical self, you will want to play such a game – touching other people to show that they are among his horizontal connections. Children can learn about the horizontal self through games that involve touching hands, standing beside, making circles of people, or drawing groups of friends or family members. The basic concept of horizontal connection is the same for your grandchild as it is for yourself. Just think about being able to reach out and to touch all the people who are in your everyday life, then think of ways in which they help you define who you are, and you will have the concept of horizontal self.

Use this space to write a short description of your *horizontal self* and the people who are in your horizontal community.

_____

_____

_____

_____

_____

_____

_____

How would you describe your "Grandpa Oak" vertical self?

Most of us never have an opportunity to answer that question, because it is seldom asked. Spirituality is often considered to be synonymous with religion and people shy away from questions about religion. The soul is often seen as a religious concept, but research has shown that anyone, religious or not, can benefit from connections that are soulful. Thomas Moore has written about the cultivating of spirituality and depth in everyday life. In his *Care of the Soul*, Moore suggests that "soul is tied to life and all its particulars" and that spirituality is revealed in attachments. Perhaps it is not accidental that we struggle and falter when we attempt to define the soul. Moore says that definition is an intellectual process and the soul prefers to imagine.

Take a few moments to allow your soul to imagine. Get comfortable. You may want to close your eyes. Imagine that your feet are anchored to the ground by a deep taproot like one that might support an ancient tree. Feel the nourishment coming into your body as if it were moving upward through this deep root. You should become aware of a vertical dimension within yourself. Once you feel your vertical dimension you can start to explore what is stored deep within yourself. In your *vertical self* you will find your spirituality and the beliefs and values that guide your actions. You will find also that place of anchoring for the most meaningful relationships of your life.

Try this exercise for your vertical self:

- Reach deep inside and pull out the feeling that you have when you are connected to other people. Find that warm, secure feeling of attachment and enjoy it. Don't think about the relationship – think about the *feeling that you get* from the relationship.

- How do you get to that feeling of attachment? What actions make you feel attached – are there hugs, certain words, songs, or memories that make you feel connected? How did your soul learn the songs that it sings?

- While you are feeling connected, think about your *vertical self*. Think about being rooted deeply. Feel the connection , the attachment, growing out of your vertical self, just as the branches of a tree grow out of connections with the root system.

Does it feel good to use all of yourself? Do you enjoy the feeling that you have when you connect with other people by drawing from your deeply rooted vertical self?

Use this space to describe your *vertical self* – the spiritual you, the rooted you – your "Grandpa Oak". As you write this description, think about the feelings that you are having.

_____

_____

_____

_____

_____

_____

_____

_____

WEEK TWO

THE LETTER:
SOUL WORK FOR GRANDPARENTS AND GRANDKIDS

Doing soul work is an individual occupation. You are the only person who can look into your soul. The journey into your vertical self will be yours alone. But what you find deep inside yourself can and will be shared with those who you choose to invite into your circle. More importantly, you can teach your grandchild how to go deeply into the soul and to connect from soulful groundings. Imagine how wonderful it would be to get a letter someday from your grandchild saying, "Pop-pop, guess what! I have met the most wonderful woman. She is my soul mate. I love her from the deepest place in my heart. She is the only person who has ever really understood me – besides you. I want you to know that she and I talk about feelings, just like you and I used to talk. It feels like home. I love you." You can do it. You can give your grandchild the gift of connection. You can fill his life, strengthen his marriage, and bless his children – if you help him find the road to his own soul.

THE LETTER – PART ONE

Use the space provided to write a letter to your grandchild. Imagine her or him at age 17. Give advice about "how to handle the opposite sex." **THIS IS IMPORTANT: Write your advice as if *you* were the one who is going to be loved.** Tell your grandchild what it takes to make a person feel loved and connected, but do that from your own perspective. Talk about feelings that are real to you.

Dear _____,

If you want someone to know that you love them, try to make them feel...

_____

_____

_____

_____

_____

_____

_____

THE LETTER – PART TWO

Now, write a letter to your grandchild telling her or him how it feels to love a grandchild. Do not talk about the fact that you love your grandchild, rather describe the feelings that you have about loving your grandchild.

Dear _____,

Loving you, my grandchild, feels like _____

_____

_____

_____

_____

_____

_____

_____

WEEK THREE

THE PHONE CALL:
MORE SOUL WORK

My children grew up with polar opposites for grandparents – one set was almost embarrassingly expressive for my tastes and the other set was guarded, to say the least. Our family lived far away from both sets of grandparents and phone calls were the preferred method of communication. I remember phone calls with the expressive set of grandparents that would go on and on with giggles and endearments. Although I resisted my temptation to eavesdrop on these animated conversations, I assumed from the frequently heard squeals and "I love you's" that they usually focused on feelings. With the other set, there were discussions about the weather, schoolwork, and plans for the week to come. I sometimes imagined that when they were old enough my children would bypass these conversations and simply look up in an almanac the information that they were now getting from these grandparents. Think about what you say to your grandchild and how you say it. If you are separated from your grandchild, your contact time is especially valuable. Even if you live nearby, phone conversations can extend the precious time that you have to build connections with your grandchildren. Conversations with children serve several purposes. Through conversation, we educate children and we socialize them so that they use our language, accept our values, and adopt our expectations for their behavior. With each conversation, you have a choice to be task oriented or feelings oriented. When your grandchild hangs up the phone, what do you want her to remember?

Try this exercise for a week: make a "pretend" call to your grandchild every day and keep a record of what you say and how you say it. Are your conversations about topics or about feelings? What do you enjoy about a conversation with your grandchild? At the end of the week, take time to look over your notes and to remember the "conversations." Go back and rate each practice conversation on a scale from 1-3 according to how it made you feel (1= did not like it; 2 = cannot remember it; 3 = loved it). If your grandchild is old enough to talk on the phone and if the cost of calling is not prohibitive for you, make real calls every day for the next week and try out your preferred style with your grandchild. At the end of each call ask, "How does talking with [your grandparent name] make you feel?" If your grandchild is too young to talk on the phone, try practicing your best telephone style on his parents. What have you lost if you improve your connections with your own child and her or his partner as you wait for a chance to connect to that adorable little person who lives in their household?

TELEPHONE CONVERSATION LOG

	TOPIC	FEELINGS	RATING			NOTES
			1	2	3	
DAY 1	_____	_____	___	___	___	_____
	_____	_____	___	___	___	_____
DAY 2	_____	_____	___	___	___	_____
	_____	_____	___	___	___	_____
DAY 3	_____	_____	___	___	___	_____
	_____	_____	___	___	___	_____
DAY 4	_____	_____	___	___	___	_____
	_____	_____	___	___	___	_____
DAY 5	_____	_____	___	___	___	_____
	_____	_____	___	___	___	_____
DAY 6	_____	_____	___	___	___	_____
	_____	_____	___	___	___	_____
DAY 7	_____	_____	___	___	___	_____
	_____	_____	___	___	___	_____

WEEK FOUR

THE SOUL PACT

Do you want to be your grandchild's soul mate? Think, before you answer. Being a soul mate is a special responsibility. It means that you will listen, hear, and care. Soul mates have extraordinary relationships. They act toward each other with extraordinary consideration of feelings, beliefs, and dreams. Being a soul mate is a trust that once established must never be betrayed.

The most critical task that adults have in relating to a child during the first year of life is to gain the child's trust. Infants have a lot to learn about their environment and the people in it. For all their curiosity and desire to explore, they are frightened by sudden change or unfamiliar people. Child development experts agree that trust develops best within caring relationships with adults who are dependable, honest, loving, consistent, respectful, happy, calm, and supportive. Children interpret these characteristics as indications that the adults around them are safe and constant. Your grandchild has no way of knowing you except through your words and actions. Your feelings, along with your actions and words, become the tools which build trusting relationships with your grandchild. If you establish a trusting relationship during the first year, you are well on your way to a soulful relationship that can last a lifetime.

Here are some tips for developing trust in a young child. (Taken from "Helping Trust Happen" by A. L. Dombro in *Scholastic Pre-K Today*, Oct. 1992)
1. Be dependable.
2. Know the child as an individual.
3. Adapt your daily routines to the child's individual needs.
4. Encourage the child to participate in daily routines.
5. Provide opportunities to practice making decisions (as soon as the child is developmentally ready).
6. Use words and tones that say you care for and respect the child.
7. Handle the child's body with respect.
8. Say goodbye whenever you leave the room – do not "sneak away".
9. Create a safe environment that encourages the child to explore.
10. Take care of **you**. Remember that when your own needs are met, you are better able to meet the needs of others.

Read over these ten tips again carefully, thinking about your feelings as you read each one. For example, how do you feel about giving a child freedom to wander and explore your house or apartment? I remember going shopping with my mother and being told that I must keep my hands clasped behind my back from the moment we entered the store until we left. Today, stores provide play areas for children or shopping parents tether toddlers to leashes. Children have much more freedom to explore within safe constraints. When your grandchild comes for a visit, how do you feel about allowing her to roam freely among your treasured possessions? Trust is reciprocal. If a child feels trusted, he will be able to return that trust. Make certain that your home is safe – use childproof locks and keep weapons, kitchen utensils, and chemicals in safe storage – and then relax. Children can grow up using china or learning to touch a flower softly.

Now that you know how to foster trusting relationships with children, you can think about the special trusting relationship that you want with your grandchild. Use this exercise to design a Soul Pact for you and your grandchild. If your grandchild is an infant, say the words to him while you are rocking him or holding him close. Save the ritual until you can repeat it when you and your grandchild can participate together. Rituals are important because they mark an event as being significant. Weddings, funerals, and graduations are familiar rituals. This soul pact ritual is unique to the relationship that you and your grandchild are building. It is yours and his or hers alone. Design it for yourself. Make it special and soulful and it will be important.

THE SOUL PACT

Ritual Space: Select a quiet place where you and your grandchild will not be disturbed. Bring with you to that place any objects that signify love or trust to you and your grandchild (Examples: favorite toys or a blanket, pictures of people who love you, religious symbols). Define a space for your ritual. You may want to sit on a blanket or make a circle. Make the place feel special and set apart from the rest of your environment.

Ritual: Write in this space a description of the words and actions that make up your personal ritual. During this "ceremony" you will make clear to your grandchild your intention to be her or his soul mate. The ritual should convey your commitment to have a soulful bond, to listen and to really hear when your grandchild has a joy or sorrow to share with you. The child should participate in the ritual at a level appropriate to her or his developmental stage. You should use age-appropriate language that your grandchild will understand. Perhaps the child will do something as simple as to offer you a piece of cookie or to say "I love you." You may say something as simple as "I will love you forever and always be here for you." The point is for both you and your grandchild to recognize formally that your relationship is special and extraordinarily meaningful to both of you.

Our ritual will be: _____

_____

_____

_____

_____

_____

Reflection: When you are alone, think about the ritual.

What were your feelings?_____

_____

_____

_____

_____

How did your grandchild respond?

_____

_____

_____

_____

_____

_____

What do you intend to do to keep your Soul Pact with your grandchild?

_____

_____

_____

_____

_____

_____

Your grandchild represents a new generation. Besides loving your grandchild and having a relationship with her, what will you do to connect your generation to hers?

_____

_____

_____

_____

_____

Congratulations! You have begun one of the most significant relationships of your life.

You are also part of a growing alliance of people committed to making a difference in the lives of grandparents and grandchildren. You are a participant in the most important family relationship of the new millennium. You and other grandparents like you are committed to making the world a better place by Connecting the Generations!

THE WORLD OF A CHILD

It's a small world after all;
It's a small world after all;
It's a small world after all;
It's a small, small world.
    – Robert & Richard Sherman, 1964

The world of a child is filled with wonder and change. Everywhere there are new things to experience and new concepts to learn. The development of language skills alone is a small miracle, and there is so much more. The human brain is a great sorter of information – keep this, file that, sense this, feel that. Constantly the senses are receiving signals and actions are being chosen. Have you ever thought about the wonder of it all? Your infant grandchild is hearing your voice and assigning some meaning to the sounds that you make, without the benefit of a fully developed vocabulary. Then the child is responding in some way, without the benefit of fully developed sensory, muscular, or skeletal systems. In spite of limitations, your grandchild manages to navigate through the murky waters of communication and to thrill you with well-timed smiles, gurgles, sighs, and gestures that convince you that her knowledge far exceeds her stage of physical development.

From the beginning of life, your grandchild has interacted with his environment. I look back on the first few days of my children's lives and see traits that are in them today as they finish college and launch careers. Within hours of their births I knew that my son passionately objected to things that do not work according to his expectations and that my daughter preferred continuity over change. How did I know? My son shrieked and thrashed about when his milk supply – the breasts of a nervous young mother – failed to deliver upon demand. My daughter wanted simply to cuddle in the same position for hours on end. By the time both children came home from the hospital, they had made me aware of these preferences and I am certain that I treated them accordingly as I brought them into their new home environment. Even very young children help to shape their environment while at the same time being influenced by that environment.

Ideally, children and their environments work together to produce positive growth experiences. Child development specialist Urie Bronfenbrenner has suggested that the child's world is like a number of concentric circles. Closest to the child and most directly influential on his behavior are parents, brothers and sisters, neighborhood play groups, school friends, and church. Beyond this closest level, the child experiences the social world in a more indirect way through contacts with extended family such as uncles and aunts, friends of the family, neighbors, service providers, and the influences of radio and television. The most abstract influence on the child comes from the attitudes and ideologies of the culture into which the child is born.

Grandparents often worry about their grandchildren growing up in a culture with different values than the ones which the grandparents remember from their own childhood. Music, clothes, and hairstyles symbolize differences between the generations in our society. Families have serious arguments over ear piercing and the loudness of a stereo. These disagreements draw battle lines between the generations in a family. I think it is important to know what is really happening when a family fights over generational symbols such as these. When you consider some simple principles of child development, you may see that some of the "problems" you fear are no more than "phases" which can be managed with loving guidance of the child and the passage of time.

As children develop, they want to explore the world beyond their family environment. The two year old says "No" to everything because he is trying to exert independence. He wants to see how much he can do by himself. In a younger child, actions do not usually constitute a challenge to parental authority. He will go pick flowers in the neighbor's yard just because they are pretty and he wants them.

However, the four year old is beginning to feel uncomfortable with her dependency. She is ready to be part of a larger social sphere. If comformity is usually expected of her, she may want to pick the flowers in the neighbor's yard just to see if she can get by with breaking a rule.

Things get really complicated by the time the child reaches adolescence because now the signals are mixed. On the one hand, parents, grandparents, teachers, and other authority figures are voicing expectations that the adolescent will "grow up". In direct contrast to that message are restrictions that are imposed on the adolescent's behavior, partially because adults are concerned about the adolescent and partially because these adults are struggling with their own ambivalent feelings about letting go the precious child. It is important for parents and grandparents to examine our own feelings. Why is a particular restriction important – does it make us feel better or is it good for the adolescent? I think we often forget that we as parents and grandparents are developing right along with our children and grandchildren. Transitions for the child trigger complementary transitions for the adults who love them. The family is a system. Change in one individual creates change in the whole system. Many interdependencies comprise the family environment, just as animals, plants, and the elements comprise ecosystems in the natural environment. Connections – our world is all about connections!

Let's get back to you and your grandchild. With all that is going on in the world outside your family environment, you will still have an enormous influence on your grandchild. Dr. Urie Bronfenbrenner and others who have studied carefully the development of young children are convinced that the experiences that a child has within the family are by far the most important in the child's life. The home, school, or day care environments in which your grandchild spends every day are vital to his development. Family influence can go with the child to day care or school if the family stays involved. Going with your child or grandchild into a day care or school classroom can help him to build a bridge from home to the new environment. Volunteering in your grandchild's school or day care center can show him that you care about his world. Your grandchild needs to feel your support, no matter where he is. The influences of a loving family – including your influence as a grandparent – are what shapes your grandchild's attitudes, beliefs, and behaviors. A loving family environment can subdue the influences of a hostile world outside.

WEEK ONE

THE FAMILY ENVIRONMENT

The first exercise in this chapter is designed to help you to see the influences that may be available to your grandchild within her family environment. Who are the people who will have frequent contact with your grandchild? What are their skills, interests, and beliefs? Let's test your knowledge of those who will influence your grandchild. At the top of the chart are five categories of adults who are in your grandchild's social environment. Fill in the cells with names of people who will have frequent contact with your grandchild – those who will see or talk with him at least three times per week. Give yourself the designated points for accurate knowledge that you have about each person within each category regarding their career/education, talents/skills, life goals, religion/politics, and feelings about relationships. You may want to make some phone calls or write some letters in order to verify your answers.

Here is an example of a completed row of cells.

	PARENTS	GRAND-PARENTS	TEACHERS/ PAID CARE GIVERS	EXTENDED FAMILY	CLOSE FAMILY FRIENDS
CAREER/ EDUCATION	100 points ea. Dad=Teacher B.A. Mom=Artist M.A.	100 points ea. GF=Retired Military; H.S. GM=Teacher B.A.	100 points ea. Baby Sitter ??? (no points)	100 points ea. None with frequent contact	100 points ea. Neighbor= Salesperson; Education unknown

Fill in the cells with as much information as you have or can obtain. Remember, these are the people who will help to shape your grandchild's attitudes and beliefs. These people will have strong influences on that little person who is so important to you. When you finish filling in all the cells, total your points for your score. Give yourself the designated point credit for having correct information about each person within a category. For example, correct information about the parents in the sample above gave us 200 points (100 points for each parent). Of course, the real reward is in getting to know the people who will influence your grandchild's beliefs and life choices.

THE FAMILY ENVIRONMENT

Inside each cell, write in the names of people who will influence your grandchild. Write in a few words that describe these people and the influence that you expect them to have. For example: Mom=Roman Catholic=strong religious beliefs. Total your credit points for each column. Give yourself the points indicated for each person within a category about whom you give accurate information. You will note that points get higher toward the bottom of this grid. The reason is that you will need to know the person better to know their "feelings about relationships" than to know their "career/education".

	PARENTS	GRAND-PARENTS	TEACHERS/ PAID CARE GIVERS	EXTENDED FAMILY	CLOSE FAMILY FRIENDS
CAREER/ EDUCATION	100 points ea.	100 points ea.	100 points ea.	100 points ea.	100 points ea.
TALENT/ SKILLS	200 points ea.	200 points ea.	200 points ea.	200 points ea.	200 points ea.
LIFE GOALS	300 points ea.	300 points ea.	300 points ea.	300 points ea.	300 points ea.
RELIGION/ POLITICS	400 points ea.	400 points ea.	400 points ea.	400 points ea.	400 points ea.
FEELINGS ABOUT RELATION-SHIPS	500 points ea.	500 points ea.	500 points ea.	500 points ea.	500 points ea.

Sum your points for each column. _____   _____   _____   _____   _____

Your total: _____

Compare your column totals to see where you have the most or least knowledge. Remember, the more you know about the influences other people have on your grandchild, the more you can help her by filling in the gaps with your own wisdom and influence.

WEEK TWO

"HE GOT HIS _____ FROM ME!"

You cannot influence every aspect of your grandchild's life. You have choices to make in influencing your grandchild. There must be some skill or belief or feeling that you like so much about yourself that you want to pass it on to your grandchildren. Maybe it is something that you wish your child had "inherited" – playing the piano like you or sharing your religion. Use this space to record the one thing that you would like your grandchild to gain from your influence on his life. Then make some notes about what actions you might take in order to increase your influence on your grandchild's choices in this area. For example, if you want to influence your grandchild to play the piano, will you pay for lessons or buy a piano for practicing?

_____

_____

_____

_____

_____

_____

_____

_____

_____

_____

_____

_____

_____

_____

_____

_____

_____

_____

_____

WEEK THREE

Your Grandchild and the Natural Environment

Now, I would like for you to go with me beyond the home and family environment into the natural environment in which we all live and grow. Biologists, geographers, sociologists, and anthropologists who study the interaction of people with their natural environments have found that our emotional and social well-being as well as our health can be connected to our physical surroundings. You may be skeptical, wondering, "What does this have to do with grandparents? Why would she be talking about 'tree-huggers' in the midst of a discussion about my grandchild's development?" Hang in there. This is all about connections.

Sociologists and anthropologists, such as Steve Picou and his colleagues who have studied the impact of man-made disasters on Alaskan fishing villages, have found that oil spills or chemical contaminations that have killed fish and other wildlife have dire consequences for humans as well. Following the Exxon-Valdez oil spill of 1989, villagers around Prince William Sound where the most environmental damage was done suffered depression, break-ups of marriages and communities, suicides, and other stress related problems. People who are closely bound by their occupations to their environments are deeply affected emotionally when those environments are harmed. In fact, many communities that depend on fishing or hunting also place high priority on building sustainable environments that maintain their interdependent relationships with wildlife that share their physical space.

Think about your grandchild's world. You can create a sustainable environment for your grandchild. You can help to make her world stable, predictable, and constant over time and in doing so give her a context in which it is safe to learn, to trust, and to love. While you are creating this safe and sustainable environment for your grandchild, you can teach him how we use our skills to create a sustainable environment for future generations. Your grandchild will see your concern about the way our earth's resources are treated. She will also see your concern about the home environment in which she lives. Children accept interdependence in their families and in their world. Sometimes they teach the adults around them important lessons about the host of connections that surround us.

I recently spent a week with my daughter, who lives in a house with four other environmental sciences majors at a large Eastern university. One day during my visit, I noticed something over the light fixture in the bathroom. Drawing back my hand to swat it, I asked, "Is that a spider?" Kate stopped my impulse to kill and said, "Here in this house we coexist with the insects that are not dangerous." Besides making me feel like a potential murderer whose violent intentions had just been thwarted, her comment made me reflect on my feelings about my environment and hers.

I was not surprised at Kate's choice of a career in environmental economics. That choice, as well as many others that she has made, came from the influences of her parents and grandparents and from her home environment. When Kate was less than three years old, she and I were working in my flower garden, a favorite place for both of us. I noticed that she had managed to contort her body so that her face was on the ground. "What are you doing?" She looked up at me with a big smile and dirt around her mouth and answered, "Kissing that worm." No one had told her that earthworms were not kissable creatures. No one had spoiled her feelings of unity with other species in her environment. Perhaps she had her grandfather's spirit. Her favorite photo of my dad was an image of him with a wild bird perched trustingly on his fingers. How quietly grandparents find their way into the fabric of a grandchild's life – and there they stay...forever!

MY HOUSE...YOUR HOUSE

This activity is appropriate for a grandchild who is two years old or older. If your grandchild is an infant, use this exercise yourself to explore your own feelings so that some day you can discuss with your grandchild the significance of his surroundings in making him who he is.

All creatures in our world have some kind of habitat that provides food, water, shelter and space. Our needs vary dramatically regarding our habitats. Often, the construction of a human habitat disturbs the habitats of other animals. Children can learn much about the essentials of living when they are engaged in conversations about "animal houses" and "people houses." This kind of conversation may also provide a good context for teaching your grandchild certain safety information, such as his home address or how to contact help in case there is an emergency in his household.

Find a place where you can talk to your grandchild with his full attention. Some appropriate places are: a front porch, a warm and friendly kitchen, or any quiet but comfortable place in your house or yard.

Start the conversation as, "I like living in my house. In my house, I have food to eat, water to drink, a roof to keep me warm in the winter and dry when it rains. My favorite place in my house is _____ because when I am there I can _____ _____.
Tell me about your house." (Be sure that your grandchild has the opportunity to discuss the basic needs that are met in our habitats and also that he tells you something about his own space within the place where his family lives. It is important for him to have a place to call his own, no matter how many other people share the house or apartment in which he lives.)

Next, give your grandchild an opportunity to compare human habitats with animal habitats. This is all part of teaching the child that all of the animals in the environment share a planet and are connected to each other in many ways. Start this part of your conversation as, "My house is not very much like a turtle's house. Where does a turtle go when he goes home?" (Encourage your grandchild to compare the turtle's house to yours.) "But, you know what? A turtle uses his house for some of the same things that I get from my house. Do you know what those things are?" (Let your grandchild guess, but be sure that he mentions at least that the turtle gets shelter and a space to call his own from his "house." Then talk about sources in the turtle's habitat that provide water and food.)

Repeat this exercise using other animals. You may want to discuss the impact of human housing on the habitats of other animals. This discussion is especially interesting to grandchildren who are 6 years old or younger.

WEEK FOUR

A WORLD OF WORLDS

Children love to explore. You can use exploration to teach lessons about the connections that are all over our interdependent planet. As you connect with your grandchild, why not show her that she is connected to beings great and small who share her environment.

A short walk can be an infant's first link with the animals around him. Historically, babies in our culture as well as infants in other cultures have long enjoyed the privilege of riding on their parents' backs or shoulders, or being carried near the parents' eye level, as the parents walked or rode horses to interesting and beautiful destinations. By contrast, baby strollers and carriages introduced later blocked the infant's view of the world and put his eye level at a different place from that of the parent or grandparent. The result was that the infant saw the world from a perspective that was different from the adult's. While strollers and baby carriages are still popular and convenient for many, babies today in increasing numbers enjoy traveling on parents' backs or cradled in pouches against the chests of adults who love them. If you are physically able to carry your grandchild, you may enjoy taking him on a walk holding him on your back or chest. Your walk will be a success if your infant grandchild learns that the outdoors is a pleasant and interesting place to be.

If your grandchild is old enough to walk, your exploration of the environment takes on new dimensions. Get a small net from a toy, hardware, or pet store. Either a butterfly net or fish net will do. Take your grandchild to a pond or stream. Choose a safe place. Tell your grandchild to lie down on the bank – that will avoid any chance of her losing her balance and falling into the water. Scoop the net into the water. Help your grandchild to name all the things that are caught in the net. As your grandchild grows, you may enjoy hiking or camping together. Whatever the activity, your grandchild can learn from you that connections are everywhere in our world.

If you are a grandparent who lives far away from your grandchildren, you can plan a visit to a natural history museum, a camping trip, or a short hike when you next visit your grandchild. If visits are rare, try a mailed exchange of animal pictures. Send a picture of a rabbit to your grandchild and ask her to send you a picture of the rabbit's home. Continue these exchanges with several animals and their habitats. This should add interest to a number of your letters to your grandchild.

When you go on a nature outing of any kind with your grandchild, don't forget to take along a small notepad and pencil, or a video or audio tape recorder so you will not miss any of those precious observations that your grandchild makes. If you do not record your observations while you are on the outing, then as soon as you get home make a few notes in the space provided below. Seeing the environment through the eyes of your grandchild can open a whole new world for you. Such are the pleasures of connecting the generations.

REFLECTIONS ON NATURE OUTING

_____

_____

_____

_____

_____

_____

_____

_____

_____

_____

_____

_____

_____

_____

_____

_____

_____

_____

CHAPTER 6

ALL IN THE FAMILY

Women have been the traditional kin keepers in American families for most of our history. In most American families, women address the invitations and holiday greeting cards, they plan and prepare for family celebrations, and they keep family records. The gap between men's and women's involvement in kin keeping is closing for two reasons. Women are less available for such activities because they are more involved outside the home. Women today make up over 45% of the paid labor force. Half of all married mothers with infants under the age of one year are working. Fewer than 5% of families in America have the "Leave It to Beaver" family lifestyle in which the father works and the mother stays at home to take care of the children and tend to family obligations.

At the same time, men are increasingly interested in and available for family-related activities of all kinds. A study reported in *The American Woman* in 1988 compared married men and women who worked equal hours at their jobs and found that the women put in an additional 18 hours per week doing home and family labor, while the men spent on average 12 minutes per week in primary child care. But men's roles in families are changing as we enter the new millennium. Men are beginning to wake up and smell the diapers! Men have always been family members as well as paid workers, but there was a period in our history during which men largely abandoned their family roles in favor of success at work. Now, men are discovering their families. Home-based work, made possible by more flexible attitudes in business and by the increasingly important work role of the personal computer, has reintroduced men to the family environment. In addition, even those men who work away from home are faced with the necessity to participate in child care, elder care, and housekeeping because their working wives are simply not around to cook, clean, and meet the needs of growing children or elderly parents.

Both men and women are discovering that family traditions and rituals suffer when the adults in the family all work outside the home. The most notable ritual to go has been the family evening meal. The family dinner was once a time for family discussions that focused the family's attention on its individual members and their separate worlds and brought the family back together as a unit. Opinions, values, and accomplishments were discussed around a bountiful table. Today, each family member may grab a meal at a different fast food restaurant or children may eat at home while watching TV and parents may eat on the run between their jobs and evening commitments. I have a friend whose father required his three sons to read three different newspapers each day so the family could hear different perspectives on world events when they discussed them over family dinner. On the rare occasions when today's families find time to share a formal meal, they are apt to use the family convocation to discuss personal problems or issues in the family rather than to share perspectives on the world condition. The family meal, where it exists at all, has lost its significance in connecting the family to community and society.

Kin, tradition, and family rituals are still important elements of family life. Grandparents are often especially concerned with these links to a family's history. How can we be sure that children who grow up in the busy outer-world-oriented families of today are also grounded in their family's heritage? This chapter will help you to explore the importance of kin and tradition in your own life and to develop creative solutions that will keep kin, family values, and family traditions alive in the hearts and souls of the coming generations of your family.

Let's begin by thinking about why traditions and rituals are important in our families. Traditions are important because:

- They represent a family's history.
- They connect a family's future to its past.
- They reinforce a family's values.

Similarly, rituals are important to a family because:

- They anchor family change to family tradition.
- They provide a safe and predictable context for life's transitions.

Traditions help us to remember that our families go on over time. Think of the tradition expressed in these statements: "We always have a turkey at Thanksgiving"..."My mom bakes Christmas cookies from her grandmother's recipe"..."Of course we like big family parties – we're Italian!" Each statement is an affirmation that a particular family has both history and future. Traditions give us comfort. They help us to understand who we are and how we got to be. Family sociologists refer to this concept as *family continuity*. Every family needs a sense of permanence against which it can play the changes that occur in daily life. Without a sense of tradition, families would fall apart whenever there was a death, divorce, or for that matter, whenever a new baby came along and changed the family's structure. Family continuity is the background for the ups and downs of family life. Family traditions are the reminders that the background will always be there.

Rituals are important because they help families to celebrate change in a safe way. Rituals remind family members that the traditions – the family continuity – will not be broken by a discontinuous event. There is often a religious ritual that welcomes a baby into a family and its religious community. The ritual, or ceremony, reminds us that the family is continuous and that the new member will be accepted into the flowing river of family time. Similarly, a ritual at death, the funeral, reminds us that the family will survive the loss of a member. In fact, a funeral is perhaps the best example of a family's ability to acknowledge both change and continuity at the same moment. Eulogies often speak of a family's history and hope for the future while recognizing the loss of a valuable family member.

Perhaps the most familiar ritual in American family life is the wedding. Marriage is a tradition. Historically, U.S. marriage and family laws have been based on the premise that the husband is head of the household. Marriage placed the woman and any future children under the protection of the man. Technically, the basis of a wedding ceremony was in the beginning the need to have a ritual to mark the transfer of property – the bride – from her father to her husband. Although weddings today range in purpose from parties that celebrate romantic love to celebrations of mutual commitment and support for each other, the various traditions and rituals surrounding weddings remain linked to early notions about marriage. In any case, the families of the bride and groom contribute traditions to the ritual that unites the couple and joins their family destinies.

So far, we have talked about rituals and traditions and their meaning in family life, but we have not discussed their importance to children. Why do children need to grow up in families that have rituals and traditions? The most obvious answer is that children need continuity. They need to feel stability in their environments. They need the safety of a predictable home base. But there is more to this ritual and tradition thing than that. Family traditions are linked to family values, and children need to learn values in the context of family life. Many family rituals are connected to belief systems or values that are held by the family. For example, regular attendance at a church or involvement in a religious community is connected to the beliefs held by adults in the family. Children learn to honor and adopt those beliefs within a supportive environment. In another realm, children who enjoy a traditional summer camping trip or ritual evening walk with their parents learn that the outdoors and exercise are important to life. Children observe what is important to their parents and grandparents and they make those values part of their own lives.

By the way, if your grandchildren do not learn their values from their parents and from you, they will learn them from someone else. That sounds like a simple thought, but it is, I think, quite profound. If the non-directive, permissive parenting of the sixties taught us nothing else, it has taught us that children who do not receive guidance from their families will take direction from friends, the media, and the drug dealer on the street. Parents need not be dictators and family life need not be prison, but parents do need to know their own values and to communicate those beliefs that are important to them to children who are waiting for direction.

Hillary Rodham Clinton's book, *It Takes a Village*, is an appeal to everyone to recognize the importance of children in our society. The First Lady argues that all the adults in a society can influence the development of a child. If you turn over that rock, you will find another truth. If the "village" can influence for good, it can also influence for bad. If the "village" can work with the family, it can also work against it. Parents and grandparents who want their children to be able to make decisions that reflect the family's shared beliefs need to send those children out of the home and into a world of potential influences with a foundation of principles that are based in the family's values. Rituals and traditions anchor your grandchild to his family.

A friend of mine quit her well-paying job as a master artist for a large publishing firm when she had her first child in her late thirties. Her family struggled to make it on one salary. One day in a conversation about how life had changed since she had stopped working, she reminded me, and herself I think, "I want to recognize my children as part of me. I didn't wait this long to have children for someone else to raise." My friend was fortunate to have circumstances that allowed her to choose to stay at home. Parents who must intrust their children to the care of others can still maintain influence on their children's values. Grandparents can help as well. The key is to provide the child with clear evidence of what is important in your family. Traditions that link the present to the past and rituals that remind your grandchild that family is constant will make it easy for her to feel the strength of family bonds and the tug of family values. As the popular song reminds us, you can be the wind beneath her wings. Your family values can direct her flight.

WEEK ONE

YOUR TRADITION QUOTIENT

The first two exercises in this chapter will help you to see how important traditions and rituals are to you. Follow the directions for the exercises and you will learn just how rigid or flexible you are where traditions and rituals are concerned. I remember announcing to my family one Thanksgiving that I had decided to eliminate the traditional ham from our holiday menu and to serve only the turkey. I thought I sensed relief in the expressions of three of the four of us, who were no doubt thinking that this would be one year when we would leave the holiday meal not feeling as stuffed as the glorious bird we had just devoured. Then there was a shriek. Our daughter had realized that the family Thanksgiving dinner would be altered by this omission. I can only imagine what she would have done if I had decided to keep the ham and toss the turkey with his little white paper booties and cranberry garnish. She burst into tears and wailed, "We have always had ham and turkey. What's wrong with us this year?" The ham went back on the menu – another family tradition saved. Later in this chapter, you will learn how you as a grandparent can help everyone in your family to honor the essential traditions, rituals, and values in your family.

We are going on a scavenger hunt through the attic of your soul. Get three small boxes – any plain cardboard boxes will do – and some old magazines, a pair of scissors, and some writing paper, a pen, and an envelope. Find a comfortable chair where you can sit and cogitate. Relax and put yourself in your "memory mode."

(1) Look through the pictures in the magazines. Cut out those pictures that remind you of traditions or rituals that were important in your family when you were growing up. Put them in one of the cardboard boxes.

(2) Now go back through the magazines and find pictures that remind you of traditions and rituals that were important to you when your children were growing up. Put them in the second cardboard box.

(3) Look carefully and reflectively at the pictures in the two boxes. Select any traditions and rituals that you want to continue as your grandchildren grow up. Put those pictures in the third cardboard box.

(4) Write a letter to your grandchild telling her why you want these traditions and rituals to be as important in her life as they were in yours. Seal the letter and put it in the box with the pictures. If your grandchild is old enough to understand, then show the pictures and the letter to her the next time you see her. If your grandchild is an infant, then save your special rituals and traditions to share at a later time.

(5) If you knew that you had to let go all the traditions and rituals that have meant so much to you for all your life – except one – what would you keep? Why?

_____

_____

_____

_____

WEEK TWO

POP-POP'S LIST OF EVERYDAY VALUES AND THE RITUALS AND TRADITIONS THAT KEEP THEM STRONG

You have thought about the values that were important in your childhood and the childhood of your children. You have found your one essential value. Now, it is time to prioritize your values and to connect the most important values to the rituals and traditions that will convey them to your grandchildren.

How can you prioritize values? Politicians do it all the time; so can you. Imagine that a politically conservative grandmother gets elected to Congress. This grandmother has watched her daughter and son-in-law struggle with conflicts between work schedules and the demands of child care and she knows that her own family would benefit greatly from a bill compelling small businesses to provide leave and job guarantees for family members who need time off for child care. However, her conservative politics compel her to keep government out of business affairs. She must prioritize her values before she votes on the bill. Will she vote on her conservative political conviction that government should not regulate business policy or will she vote on her family conviction that the best care for her grandchild will come from his parent? Her decision will be based on her prioritization of values.

Use the space provided here to list the values that you hold most important. Begin with your top priority and list your values in descending order. Some examples of values that people hold are: honesty, courage, self-reliance, loyalty, kindness. You may have different values. There is no "right" list. Beside each value that you list, write a family tradition or ritual that supports that value. In the third column, write "keep" if you wish to keep that tradition/ritual for your grandchild and "change" if you wish to modify it, update it, or eliminate it. Think about why you choose the values that you choose and why you keep or change the traditions and rituals that support them.

My Values	**Traditions/Rituals**	**Change or Keep**
_____	_____	_____
_____	_____	_____
_____	_____	_____
_____	_____	_____
_____	_____	_____
_____	_____	_____
_____	_____	_____
_____	_____	_____
_____	_____	_____
_____	_____	_____
_____	_____	_____
_____	_____	_____
_____	_____	_____
_____	_____	_____

WEEK THREE

WHO'S WHO IN YOUR FAMILY

I remember taking my children to the National Archives so they could watch as their father and I made the last discovery that would link them to the genealogy of Abraham Lincoln. It was one of the worst days of our family life. Take my advice. If you get the urge to trace your family lineage, do it on your own and announce your findings to your children. Don't take them along. The only person who will get an educational experience out of that is you as you learn the value of a baby sitter. I do, however, strongly support the idea of teaching your children who are the important people in their heritage. This exercise will help you to make the rituals and traditions of your family become real to your grandchildren by linking them to real people in your family. Yes, it would have been great if I had been able to show my children Uncle Abe's picture while reminding them that freedom is an American tradition, but until my genealogical research skills are honed, I will have to settle for showing them a picture of my Aunt Leedie as she stands proudly behind the soda fountain, the first woman of her generation in our family to get a job in the city.

Somewhere in everyone's house, there is a box of pictures, or an album, or an old movie reel, or a tray of slides, that has pictures of those relatives who are not in your immediate family. My pictures of this sort are all over the house – on my dresser, in my linen drawer, in the attic. These are the pictures of relatives who had but one story that was deemed important enough to be told to me as a child. My Aunt Bess was not the warmest woman in our family, but she taught me a lot about the meaning of love for a child. Aunt Bess had twins who died at their premature birth and then a beautiful little girl made it only through her first birthday. When Aunt Bess died some 60 years later, I asked for the tiny box that contained her daughter's picture and a baby dress and shoes. My aunt had kept that box for 60 years. I wanted to know her heart and I thought I could do that by touching her daughter's things. After all, as Elizabeth Stone said, having a child "is to decide forever to have your heart go walking around outside your body." I think I understand.

When I was born, my only surviving grandparent was already in the early stages of Alzheimer's disease, but she managed to read to me and to make her mark on my life. My other grandmother had been gone for several years by the time I arrived. I have a picture of her standing in her garden and I have a lock of my father's hair folded inside a note that says in her handwriting, "E.W.'s little curls." I think about her as I tend the flowers in my courtyard. I thought of her this summer when I visited my daughter in her new house and got the tour of her newly planted flower garden. In my drawer of keepsakes, I have two envelopes, each with locks of my children's hair, and on the outside, notes in my handwriting, "Matt's first haircut" and "Kate's long hair." I know my grandmother's heart. I think I understand.

Pictures and notes are priceless treasures that families pass down over the generations. These mementoes provide connections through the visual sense and also through the heart. Use the next page for pictures of the people in your family with whom you have vital soul connections. Tell your grandchild why you selected these pictures and what these people mean to your family.

OUR FAMILY WHO'S WHO

My name is:

_____

_____

_____

I am:

_____

_____

_____

_____

My name is:

_____

_____

_____

I am:

_____

_____

_____

_____

My name is:

_____

_____

_____

I am:

_____

_____

_____

_____

My name is:

_____

_____

_____

I am:

_____

_____

_____

_____

My name is:

_____

_____

_____

I am:

_____

_____

_____

_____

My name is:

_____

_____

_____

I am:

_____

_____

_____

_____

WEEK FOUR

THE TASTE OF TRADITION

Many American traditions involve cooking and eating special foods or preparing special meals.

I wanted to share with you a recipe that your grandchild and you might enjoy making together, but my own memories of tradition are around the ritual making of dressing (stuffing for those of you above the Mason-Dixon Line) for our Thanksgiving turkey. I decided to give you my mother's recipe for Cornbread Dressing – exactly as she gave it to me. I think you will see in her language the traditions and rituals behind the recipe.

Oh yes, just so it is not a total loss for your grandchild, I am including my father's recipe for peanut butter and chocolate candy as well. This recipe has become the heart of a tradition that my daughter created. Each Christmas she honors her grandfather, who died when she was four, by making his candy as a special holiday treat.

You can modify traditions and rituals to fit your lifestyle and interests. Portable rituals are good for today's mobile families. If you must travel a long distance to be with your grandchildren on special occasions, try packing in your suitcase things that can be used in some ritual that you remember from childhood and want to keep alive with your grandchild. For example, if you like to cook with your grandchild, take along a special apron that your grandchild identifies with you. Then once you arrive at your grandchild's home, take him along on a fun shopping trip to buy the ingredients for a special traditional dish. The shopping trip will become part of the ritual that he will remember. You can talk about the tradition as you shop, building language and communication skills in your grandchild and strengthening your connection.

Try my recipes if you like. Use the space that follows them to write a special recipe from your family tradition. You and your grandchild will enjoy making your own taste of tradition.

"JOHNNIE'S CORNBREAD DRESSING"

I make a big skillet of cornbread (egg bread). Cook it till it's nice and brown. Crumble this and about three biscuits and one piece of loaf bread. Put into this, from four to six eggs (large). Wet it down with the broth from cooking of the turkey. It has to be sloppy or it will be stiff when cooked. Cut into this one medium sized onion, 1/2 blade from stalk of celery, chopped fine (that will be about 1/2 cup), salt to taste, quite a bit of sage but some people may not like it so strong. Anyway, you have a pretty good <u>taster</u> as I remember from the years past. Bake till brown. Save some broth for giblet gravy. Thicken gravy slightly, but not so it will be stiff.

"E.W.'S PEANUT BUTTER CANDY"

18 oz. jar of peanut butter; 1 cup melted oleo; 4-1/2 cups confectioner's sugar. Mix melted oleo with peanut butter, then confectioner's sugar. Pat into 13 x 9 pan. Melt 2 tsp. paraffin with 6 oz. chocolate morsels. Pour over peanut butter candy. Cut in squares.

Write your recipe in this box. Enjoy making your own traditions!

Remember, rituals and traditions are the fabric of connections between generations in your family. They anchor your grandchild in her family history. They give her a secure place in which to learn and adopt family values. Traditions and rituals help your grandchild to learn what is important to your family. They give him a sense of belonging. They reinforce family continuity. It is a good idea to be flexible and to modify your family rituals to meet the needs of changing lifestyles, but modified rituals should still be anchored in traditions that span the generations. Make it clear that you are changing the ritual because of some change in circumstance. Tell stories about the ritual as you remember it. For example, your grandfather may have hunted a wild turkey for Thanksgiving, but you buy a frozen one at the local grocery. Your grandchild will enjoy hearing about your memories. After all, the grandparent role has traditionally included being a story teller and family historian.

Your grandchild will soon develop his own memories around family rituals and traditions. How wonderful it is to watch your family continue over time. This is the joy of Connecting the Generations.

CHAPTER 7

POWER TO CONNECT

You probably do not think of your family as a political system, but you probably do grapple with issues of power in your family every day. Although most families do not hold elections or coronations, spirited debates and power struggles fill kitchens and bedrooms all over the world. Power issues in families develop around differences over the control of resources. At one time in our history, American families lived and worked together as a unit. Mothers, fathers, and children were all involved in raising crops on a small farm or hunting, fishing, and preparing food in a small village. The family that we came to know during the middle part of this century was really an anomaly. The height of this family's prevalence was during the 1950s and 1960s. Fathers left home to make money in a work place that was separated from the family's living place. Economic achievement became almost the sole measure of a man's love for his family.

Mothers were given the responsibility of home care and child rearing. The behavior and emotional well-being of the children, as well as the orderly functioning of the household, became the measure of a woman's love for her family. Since money is a recognizable resource, the control that fathers gained over the money that came into a family gave them control over many decisions about the family. For example, the father's career determined where the family lived and how much money the family had to spend. Fathers became economically powerful in the family. Mothers, on the other hand, gained power over the emotional realm of family life. The image of a mother who was able to get anything done by inducing guilt in other family members grew out of this domination by mothers over the emotions and emotional relationships of the children. Mothers became powerful in manipulating the relationships in families.

We are now experiencing a return to greater equality of men and women in family life. As more women work outside their homes, they gain more control over the family's financial well-being. Economic power in the family is equalized. As more men become involved directly in the rearing of their children, they gain more control over the family's emotional well-being. Emotional power in the family is equalized. These trends taken together mean that families have a better chance of working together as a unit for common goals. When mothers and fathers are less concerned about who has the economic or emotional edge, they can concentrate on how the family will reach its goals. Of course, during the transition period from the post World War II family to the family of today, we have seen families suffer enormous damage from strife over which adults have power and why. Especially damaging to the development of children has been the power struggles that go on between their parents over the relative status of men and women.

Many married men and women live under an uneasy truce. Each has given up something in order to live in a couple relationship. Daily battles over who takes out the trash or whose turn it is to make dinner are evidence that someone is worried about losing ground. Children watch their parents fire shots from different strongholds. They grow up observing their parents, not as a unit, but as cautious enemies living in a demilitarized zone that is called "a home."

Sometimes you see a couple that has a true "us" in which everything from shopping to love making is done by the couple and for the couple. In those phenomenal "us" relationships, individuals have managed somehow to get past the differences that we expect between men and women and to wrap their boundaries around each other. It is as if the two people have shed their individual skins and their married soul is now free to wander around inside a couple skin. I am using the word "married" to mean shared or blended. In the ideal state, married people share or blend their lives, their souls, their hopes and dreams. Issues of power fade away because the couple is always thinking and acting for the good of the married "us." Unfortunately, all couples do not attain this ideal.

If we accept as a society that it is okay for men and women who say they love each other and who are parenting the same children to act like enemies, then we set ourselves up for other kinds of family conflict as well. Parents and children have power issues. We draw lines in the sand between parents and children just as readily as we do between husbands and wives. As children grow and exert their independence, parents face their own fears about their changing roles and the loss of innocence of their children.

Some parents continue to use power as a way to control family life well into the adulthood of their children. There is another, and I believe more effective, way to manage the growth of children. If parents and children develop a family "us," they will accept each stage of the child's development as another milestone in the family's effort to launch the child as a responsible citizen of the world. I am not saying that parents should step out of their roles as teachers, guides, and disciplinarians. I am saying that parents and their children can blend their hopes and goals. Just as with the married couple that we discussed before, parents and children can include each other in the expanded boundaries of a family unit. They can walk around together in a family skin. With this perspective, the family grows as the children grow. The whole family works toward the goal of successfully moving children from dependency to autonomy.

You know, this family "us" notion is really very natural. What is unnatural is to fight with your children over their growing up. Over the years, I have had several occasions in my life to rescue baby birds who have fallen from their nests or encountered my cats upon their first journey from the nest to the world of freedom. I often put my human feelings in the bodies of the bird-mothers who have watched from high limbs as their babies tried their wings. Bird-mothers, I think, really get it! They know what parenting is all about. They nurture with a vengeance while the young birds are in the nest and then step back and expect their chicks to be successful. Bird-mothers do not need power for themselves. They need success for their children.

Grandparents get involved in power struggles in families in interesting ways. When one of my friends found out that I was writing a book about grandparenting, he reminded me of an old joke: Grandparents and grandchildren get along so well together because they are united against a common enemy. There may be more truth there than humor. Grandparents who have never resolved issues of their children's independence may use the second chance of grandparenting negatively to declare a rematch in the struggle for control over their children's decisions. Just be sure the next time you call your daughter to remind her that your granddaughter needs to wear a sweater, that you are really concerned about the temperature today and not 25 years ago when your daughter refused the sweater you offered her. Whenever you have an impulse to be a directive grandparent, stop and think, "Is this about my grandchild or my child?"

In some families, grandparents see their grandchildren as a second chance. Unhappy with the approaches that they took as parents or with the way their children turned out, these grandparents want to have a strong influence on their grandchildren. They feel that their contributions are valuable because they "know what not to do." There are at least two problems with this approach to grandparenting. The first is that it is based on the premise that the grandparent knows better what the child needs than do her parents. Unless the grandparent lives in the household with the grandchild, there is probably a lot of information about the child and her needs that is not available to the grandparent. The second problem is that this approach undermines the parent's position as authority figure in the child's life. Conflicts arise over discipline. The child learns to play her parents and grandparents against each other. A far more positive way for a grandparent to handle the feeling that a grandchild is a second chance is for the grandparent to join with the child's parents in a family "us." Grandparenting is a second chance – not a second chance to prove that you can "do it right" – but a second chance to love and to foster a child's healthy development.

Power based conflicts often arise between grandparents who love the same grandchildren. I believe that we are inclined in this society toward conflict in situations that are supposed to be loving because we are an independent people. The American dream is to achieve individual success and to maintain independence. We are unaccustomed to thinking of ourselves as being best served by the collective success of ourselves with others. Is it any wonder that grandparents have trouble viewing a new grandchild as an opportunity to work collectively with a set of in-laws for the good of the family and the child? Occasionally, each set of grandparents will see the child's birth as the firing of an opening shot in a battle to see who can have the most influence and who will be the grandchild's favorite grandparents.

Before we begin the exercises in this chapter, I want to say that I know that so far in this chapter I have implied by my language that most families have both men and women present in the household and that grandparents come in sets. I recognize that many of you may be in single parent families or you may be single grandparents. Others may be remarried and your grandchildren may have multiple sets of grandparents or some single and some married grandparents. Families are infinitely varied in structure. The principles of the family "us" can work, I believe, regardless of the configuration of the family unit. The point is to get your family to feel united in its approach to marriage or coupling, parenting, and grandparenting.

Now, we need to stop for a moment and consider two special cases of grandparenting: those grandparents who are primary caregivers for their grandchildren due to the parent's absence or inability to provide care, and those grandparents who are unable to see their grandchildren regularly due to disputes over custody or visitation rights.

Today, almost a million and a half grandparents are raising their grandchildren. You may be one of these special grandparents. You may be deeply saddened by the circumstances that put you in the parenting role again. You may feel resentment because your child has abandoned his parenting responsibilities. You may be worried about your rights or how to secure the resources that you need to care for your grandchild. You may have ambivalent feelings – worrying about your child as well as being concerned about your grandchild. There are many sources of help for grandparents who find themselves in a parenting role. Two of the best resources that I have found are these:

AARP Grandparent Information Center
601 E Street, NW
Washington
DC 20049

The Brookdale Foundation Group
126 East 56th Street
New York
NY 10022

An excellent book on grandparents raising grandchildren was written by Marianne Takas and published by the Brookdale Foundation Group. The book is filled with tips that help grandparents to find the services that they need and to connect with agencies and sources of financial aid. I like the approach that Takas takes in the book, focusing on families that focus on their children. She presents many stories of grandparents who fill their grandchildren's needs for care but continue to be open to rebuilding the family if there is evidence of change in the children's absent parents. The picture is one of hope and family unity.

If you are a grandparent caregiver, you may want to get involved in a support group. The AARP Grandparent Information Center can provide guidelines for starting such a group. Many churches, family counseling centers, and senior activity centers also have information about support groups for grandparents who are parenting again. The Area Agency on Aging in your area may be able to provide referrals for services that will help you. It is difficult to focus on a family "us" when your family has been torn apart by disputes over custody or visitation of a grandchild. I want to encourage you to keep your goals clear and to remember the well-being of the child and the continuity of your family if you find yourself facing such difficult situations. The tasks of taking care of yourself through stressful times and getting information that will help you to find solutions are of primary importance. Your own future and the future of your family are at stake. This may be difficult to accept, but it is true that the process of your response is just as important as the outcome. No matter what happens regarding custody or visitation, your grandchild will remember how you behaved during the battles. She will come to know you as a grandmother or grandfather whose love shows through adversity or she will remember your bitterness and hostility. If you approach family disputes as problems that "we" must solve, your grandchild will never lose sight of the connection that holds him to his family groundings. You can give your grandchild the gift of good memories of a family that works through its problems. Nothing is more important than the well-being of your dear grandchildren. Focus on your connection with them and their connection with your family, and you can make it through.

Here are some resources on the Internet that provide information for grandparent caregivers and to grandparents who are concerned about their rights.

http://members.aol.com/GranyAnie/grg.html
Online support group for grandparents raising grandchildren

http://www.eclypse.com/GrandsRuS/
Information and support for grandparents and grandchildren

http://www.divorcenet.com
Bulletin board, forums, and chat on grandparent issues and other issues related to divorce

http://rainforest.parentsplace.com/dialog/get/grandparents2.html
Open discussion for parents, grandparents, and children

Some interesting and helpful printed resources for grandparents in general and for grandparent caregivers are:

Bengtson, V.L. & Robertson, J. (Eds.) (1985) *Grandparenthood.*
Beverly Hills: Sage.

Cherlin, A. & Furstenberg, F. (1986).
The New American Grandparent: A Place in the Family, A Life Apart.
New York: Basic Books.

Kornhaber, A. (1996). *Contemporary Grandparenting.*
Thousand Oaks, CA: Sage

Kornhaber, A. (1994). *Grandparent Power.* New York: Crown

Minkler, M. & Roe, K.M. (1993).
Grandmothers as Caregivers: Raising Children of the Crack Cocaine
Epidemic. Newbury Park: Sage.

Takas, M. (1995).
Grandparents Raising Grandchildren: A Guide to Finding Hope and Help.
Available from the National Foster Parent Association, 9 Dartmoor Drive, Crystal Lake, IL 60014.

The two exercises that follow will help you to determine your own feelings about power and conflict. Then we will focus in the last two exercises of the chapter on your grandchild and on building a family "us" as an environment for his development.

WEEK ONE

THE LADY OR THE TIGER?

Do you remember the story about a warrior who had to choose between two doors? Behind one was his lady love and behind the other was a vicious tiger? Our daily choices are not always so obvious, but they are just as real. Read the following scenarios and write your own endings for each. Write one high-conflict ending and one low-conflict ending. Which ending do you prefer? Be honest with yourself about this. If you prefer the higher conflict ending, think about what feelings you may be tapping and why they surface now. Is there an unresolved conflict that you need to address?

Story #1

Your first grandchild is turning two next week. Her mother, your daughter, is thinking of taking a new job that would require travel. When you asked her what were the plans for the toddler, she assured you that she would not take the job until she was certain that she could maintain quality child care. You are still worried. Your grandchild's father is an artist who has a flexible work schedule. However, he travels to art shows and workshops from time to time. You are the only grandparent who lives within 50 miles of the young family. You work full time, you have an active social life, and you do volunteer work. You have decided to call your daughter and invite her to lunch so you can talk out your concerns about this job decision. What do you do next?

(A) High-conflict ending...

_____
_____
_____
_____
_____
_____
_____
_____
_____

(B) Low-conflict ending...

_____
_____
_____
_____
_____
_____
_____
_____
_____

Story #2

Your 17-year-old son's girlfriend is pregnant. Your son has just told you that he does not intend to get married, but he does want to give the child his name – your family name. The girl's mother plans to raise the baby. You have met her only once and you did not like her. You are furious! You feel that the pregnancy was a ploy to get him into a bad marriage and that this decision about the baby's name is simply "Plan B." You have made it clear that abortion or adoption seem to you to be the best choices. How do you respond to your son's decision about the name?

(A) High-conflict ending...

_____

_____

_____

_____

_____

_____

_____

_____

_____

_____

(B) Low-conflict ending...

_____

_____

_____

_____

_____

_____

_____

_____

_____

_____

Story #3

Your grandson is visiting for the weekend. You want to take him shopping on Saturday to get clothes for the new season and then you want to play golf Sunday while his grandmother entertains him. Your wife, "Ms. Mother Nature" as you call her, wants to plan a camping trip for the three of you for the whole weekend. You had hoped to discover that your grandson was allergic to fresh air, but so far no luck on that score. How do you decide on the weekend's plans?

(A) High-conflict ending...

_____

_____

_____

_____

_____

_____

_____

_____

_____

_____

(B) Low-conflict ending...

_____

_____

_____

_____

_____

_____

_____

_____

_____

_____

Look back over these stories and the endings that you wrote. Answer the following questions about your power issues and your conflict management style.

Are there any unresolved power issues that you recognized as you responded to the stories? If so, how do you plan to address them?

_____

_____

_____

_____

_____

_____

How do you feel when you think about conflict in your family – angry, afraid, powerful, sad? Write your feelings here.

_____

_____

_____

_____

_____

_____

Which is most important to you – standing up for what you think is right or keeping "peace" in your family? Why?

_____

_____

_____

_____

_____

Do you anticipate any power struggles over your grandchild? If so, who will be your chief opponent? How will you handle the conflict?

_____

_____

_____

_____

_____

WEEK TWO

POWER PLAYS THAT REALLY WORK!

The trouble with most power plays in families is that they do not accomplish anything except the continuation of old roles and old interaction patterns. If your family struggles with power issues that may have an impact on your relationship with your grandchild, a little preventive action may be in order. A good model for addressing family power in decision making is the Quaker model of consensus building. In a Quaker meeting, all opinions are heard and no decision is made until everyone can bond with the decision. This does not mean that the final decision is exactly what each member of the meeting might have originally proposed. It does mean that the decision is one that each member can live with in peaceful community spirit.

If you want to manage conflict over your grandchild, begin by finding out how you might avoid it. Much of the conflict that surrounds child rearing comes from adults' differences of opinion about what are desirable outcomes for the child. You may avoid conflict if you know up front what are the family goals for your grandchild's behavior and life choices. How do your goals differ from those of the child's parents or other grandparents? Let's find out.

Take a survey of the people in your family who will have decision making influence in your grandchild's life. Usually, this group includes parents and grandparents, but it may be different in your family. Collect your information from the people who will be directly involved in your grandchild's life. Get a commitment for cooperation if you can. At the end of your survey, you will know what are likely to be the major issues as well as where are potential sources of conflict. That knowledge puts you way ahead. You can then open a discussion around possible differences and power issues. This strategy puts you well on your way to a peaceful interaction with other principals in your grandchild's life.

Who are the people who will make decisions for your grandchild or have influence on his decisions?

_____   _____

_____   _____

_____   _____

_____   _____

_____   _____

_____   _____

Make phone calls or write letters to obtain answers from each of the people listed above. Record their answers in a small notebook that you can keep. Ask these questions:

• What are your most important goals for [grandchild's name]?

• How do you think we can best work together to achieve those goals?

• I would like us to make a pact to talk to each other whenever we disagree and to try to resolve any differences over our goals for [grandchild's name].

WEEK THREE

WHAT'S IT ALL ABOUT?

You have completed two exercises. The first helped you to get in touch with your own feelings about power and potential conflict. The second helped you to begin talking to those people in your family with whom you might experience conflict over things that are important in your grandchild's life. Now we are going to turn the spotlight on your grandchild.

We looked first at your own issues of power and strategies for conflict management because you needed to resolve them in order to clear the way for concentrating on your grandchild. Remember, you and your grandchild are growing together! In confronting your own power issues, you develop a better understanding of autonomy and independence as child-rearing goals. Your job as an adult in the life of your grandchild is to work your way out of a job. Think about that. If you and the other adults are successful in giving your grandchild the skills and values that she needs, someday, you can step aside and watch her perform as a responsible, autonomous adult in her own right. Just like the bird-mother, you can watch her fly and you can know that your family values are the wind beneath her wings.

Here are some steps that will help you to foster autonomy and responsibility in your grandchild. This is where you are headed. If your family "us" is successful, you will produce a child who is grounded in the love of his family but autonomous in his decisions. Your grandchild will know how to use whatever power he has as an individual to continue to be part of your family "us." As in earlier chapters, this list of tips on child development was compiled by Nancy Jones, Child Development Specialist, teacher, and member of the National Association for the Education of Young Children.

HELPING TO BUILD AUTONOMY
Talk to the child about himself.
Point out to the child what she can do or is doing.
Give the child supervised time alone.
"Childproof" your household. Prepare it so the child can be as independent as possible.
Allow the child to do for herself whatever she can.
Praise and reinforce what the child does well immediately after it is done.
Encourage the child to do lots of things, to be active and interactive.
Give the child choices and allow her to make them whenever possible and safe.
Protect without being over-protective.

Now, it is your turn. Look at the chart above. Think about your grandchild's developmental level. Design a game or activity that will help your grandchild to be as autonomous as is appropriate for his age and developmental level. Try it the next time you are with your grandchild.

The next time I am with my grandchild, I will help him to show his autonomy by encouraging him to:

_____

_____

_____

_____

_____

_____

Think about how it makes you feel for your grandchild to be autonomous. Is it a little frightening? How difficult do you think it will be for you to let go when the time comes?

Describe your feelings here.

_____

_____

_____

_____

_____

_____

_____

_____

_____

Someday, you may be old and dependent and need your grandchild to help take care of you. Your roles will be reversed. How do you think you will feel about depending on your grandchild for personal care? Describe your feelings here.

_____

_____

_____

_____

_____

_____

_____

_____

_____

WEEK FOUR

BUILDING A FAMILY "US"

Families have different styles of decision making, managing conflict, and showing love. If your grandchild is an infant, he cannot participate in family meetings to decide on the best destination for a family vacation. He will not take sides or offer suggestions during a family argument. However, you can help even your infant grandchild to feel part of a family "us" that will be the context for his decision making and conflict management skill development. This next exercise can be scaled up or down to fit your family's needs and resources.

Plan a vacation with grandparents and parents and grandchildren all together for at least a weekend. Choose the style and destination that fits your family's interests and budget. Be sure to include the steps given here in your vacation activities. Keep a journal of your feelings during the planning stages as well as the vacation itself. Have fun!

1. Include everyone in the planning of the vacation – this means everyone – men, women, children, and the baby!

2. Make notes so you can remember your decision making process. Who made the suggestions? Who made the decision? How was the final decision reached?

3. Share everything! Make sure that everyone in the family does her part. Especially, make sure that everyone shares in the joys and responsibilities of holding and caring for the baby. Your infant grandchild will sense being nurtured by the family "us." This is his first exposure to what a united family really is.

4. Write in your journal every day. Share your thoughts and feelings with other family members and encourage them to share as well.

5. Make pictures and write notes on the backs of the pictures.

Children learn from your life. They see from your actions how autonomy and consensus both contribute to successful family life. If your grandchild sees a world of power plays and conflict, then her life is likely to be power based as well. If she sees a family "us" in which family goals are clear and family members are committed to each other's success and to the success of their children, then she will connect to that family. Connecting the Generations means fostering in ourselves and in our children a cooperative spirit, committed to the good of our families and our society. There is the real power – the power to connect!

REFLECTIONS ON OUR FAMILY VACATION

The Decision: _____

_____

_____

_____

_____

The Place:_____

_____

_____

_____

_____

Memories: _____

_____

_____

_____

_____

The Picture

CHAPTER 8

YOU AND YOUR GRANDCHILD IN THE HOUSE OF MIRRORS

Do you remember Freddie Prinz? He was a bright young Hispanic comedian whose star rose quickly in the 1960s. When I was in my teens, I thought he was one of the funniest and best looking men around. His appeal reached across ages so that he was one of the few entertainers that I enjoyed along with my parents, who were in their mid-sixties. Then one day, it was all over. Prinz had shot himself in a senseless game of chance with a friend watching. I remember thinking that he must have had no idea what he was worth or how many people loved his humor, or he would have never taken chances with his life.

How many people have we watched rise to fame or fortune, only to find out later that they never felt happy or fulfilled. Two of the most tragic stories of our time have been remembered in the original version and the rewrite of Elton John's "Candle in the Wind." Marilyn Monroe was by any standards one of the most beautiful women in American popular cultural history. Yet her biographers say that she never liked the way she looked. Diana, Princess of Wales, lived a modern fairy tale and touched the lives of millions with her grace, charm, warm spirit, and vulnerability. But if you look at pictures of Diana performing her royal duties during her time with Prince Charles, you see a face filled with sadness and desperation. How can these glamorous and famous people be so unhappy? How can their faces reflect images so different from the ones held in the hearts of fans and admirers? The answer lies in their feelings about themselves. Somehow, the adoration of millions failed to elevate the feelings that these famous people had about themselves.

How we think of ourselves is a composite of our internal feelings and the external cues that we take from people around us. The development of a child's self-concept depends on his perception of other people's feelings about him as well as on his awareness of his own body and spirit. The two essential tasks of childhood related to self-concept are:

(1) The child must learn to place some value on himself, and
(2) The child must understand how she is viewed by others.

If the child fails in either task, problems will occur in relating to other people. If the child places low value on himself, he will settle for less than happiness, perform at a level lower than his ability, and lack motivation and assertion skills. If the child cannot interpret cues about how she is perceived by others, she may not be successful at work and she may have trouble finding happiness in family relationships. You can help your grandchild to develop an accurate picture of himself. You can help him see his worth and his potential.

As a child develops, she learns that society expects that she take on certain roles and the behaviors that are associated with them. Dolls are important childhood toys in many cultures. In this country, we expect that children will treat dolls in much the same way that we treat children. When a child is given a doll, she is expected to behave toward it as if she were a parent. Children learn from our reactions to their doll play what we think are the appropriate behaviors of parents toward their children. Five-year-old Angie was suspended from kindergarten because she pulled the heads off three dolls. The teacher's disciplinary actions sent messages to Angie, her parents, and the other children in the class that violence toward children, as represented by the dolls, is inappropriate and intolerable. In contrast, our society sent a collective message to children who acquired Cabbage Patch Dolls in the early 1980s. Those young "parents" were rewarded for taking their doll children seriously enough to fill out adoption papers and give birthday parties and generally to parent their inanimate wards. We reward our children when they give us evidence that they have accepted our ideas about who they should be and how they should behave, now as children and in the future as adults.

One of the early elements of your grandchild's self-esteem is his perceived competence. In order for him to feel competent, your grandchild must have a general sense of self worth as well as an age-appropriate level of skill in getting along socially, thinking and reasoning, and performing physical activities. You can help by talking to your grandchild about his accomplishments, physical appearance, behavior, and place in the family. Sometimes parents and grandparents fail to realize that even very young children can understand positive feedback. Adults may misinterpret a child's shyness, for instance, as "just the way he is" when they could help to bring a shy child out of his shell through appropriate praise and attention that would raise the child's self-esteem. Here are some tips on handling shyness from our child development expert, Nancy Jones, member of the National Association for the Education of Young Children.

REPLACING SHYNESS AND TIMIDITY WITH APPROPRIATE FEELINGS OF SELF -WORTH

- Timidity goes hand-in-hand with low esteem and feelings of unworthiness.

- If parents or grandparents are frequently critical, children do not develop a basic belief in themselves. Children need to feel that they are good and lovable just for themselves.

- If a parent or grandparent withdraws affection as punishment, children may become afraid to act, fearing to make a mistake or fearing to take risks that might make them lose the love of an important person.

- Parents and grandparents have the power to change a child's self-esteem or self-image by influencing it positively or negatively.

- Children need to practice social situations with the help of an adult and in a safe environment.

- Parents and grandparents need to give children opportunities to speak for themselves and then praise them for communicating their feelings, desires, and ideas effectively.

- Children need a broad range of experiences so that they become confident in themselves in many circumstances and they become adaptable.

- The ability to realistically assess herself may help to build a child's self-esteem. Parents and grandparents can help a child to develop an appropriate sense of accomplishment by praising the child's behavior and accomplishments when they are age appropriate. This implies that the parents and grandparents need to know something about the child development process.

- It will not help to build a child's self-esteem to compare his behavior or ability to another child. Noting the child's progress, or comparing her current achievement level with her past, may help if it is done positively and with love.

- Watch sibling relationships! Avoid allowing a child to become the brunt of a sibling's jokes or pranks.

- Find out what your grandchild can do really well. Encourage her to excel in that activity. Praise the child and point out her strengths and accomplishments.

- Ask your grandchild to tell you what he likes best about himself. Listen carefully. When possible, agree with him about things that you notice and like.

Your grandchild's self-esteem is important, but yours is as well. Many adults experience a change in their image of themselves as they approach later life. At the heart of this change is a reorientation in the way we think about our lives. Gerontologists Bernice Neugarten and Daniel Levinson have done research on the changes that occur in mid-life. Their work shows us that at some point, we begin to think of our lives in terms of the time left before we die rather than the time spent since we were born. This change produces a feeling of urgency in many people – a need to accomplish everything for which they had ever planned or hoped. Lives are reevaluated and accomplishments are measured against goals. We call this period the "mid-life crisis." Some people make dramatic changes at this time. They go back to school, change careers, get divorces, or move to new locations. A new self emerges, ready for the rest of life. Most people handle this reorientation in mid-life less than dramatically. They do not change their lives, but they change the level of commitment that they feel to themselves, their families, or their jobs and communities. Good examples of the less dramatic approach to resolution of the mid-life crisis are planning a ceremony to renew wedding vows or making a commitment to a health and fitness program.

You may have become a grandparent right in the middle of your mid-life confrontation with your goals and dreams. The role of grandparent may be just one more reminder that you are not as young as you once were. I want to encourage you to make the grandparenting experience positive for yourself. Capture the wonder of your grandchild. After all, what is more contagious than a child's excitement with life? Having a grandchild does not make you old. There are plenty of 35-year-old grandparents in America today. In fact, the average age of an American grandparent is 45 years. Your grandchild can help you to feel younger if you will allow her to bring out the child inside you. Watch her inquisitive exploration of the world and then go do some exploring of your own. Copy her enthusiastic love for life and the people around her. My guess is that you will find your spirit renewed.

Just as your grandchild's developing self-image comes partly from the inside and partly from outside cues, your changing self-image at mid-life is related both to your internal self-awareness and to the changes in how others see you. Women after menopause are viewed differently in our society than are women of child-bearing age. Men and women in retirement often find that the loss of their work roles makes them feel different about themselves.

In many ways, developing our self-image is like walking through a house of mirrors. We know who we are, how we look, and how we feel about ourselves. However, as we go along in life, we see reflections of ourselves in the perceptions that other people have of us. Somehow, we must sort and decide which images we will keep. Out of all the cues – those that come from inside ourselves and those that come from the outside world – we form a self-image and a sense of self-esteem or self-value. Psychologist Erik Erikson proposed that in the end we either feel that we have lived our lives with integrity, having been the person that we wanted to be, or we feel despair because the process is over and our life was not our own.

The first two exercises in this chapter will help you to examine your own self-esteem and the development of self-worth in your grandchild. Remember that your grandchild's self-image is changing as he learns more about himself and how to take cues from his environment. Your own self-image may be more stable and more difficult to change if you feel the need to do so. However, if you find that you have a poor self-image, you can make changes with commitment and persistence. Watch for signs of depression or other more serious problems that may emerge in mid-life. If you cry a lot, have trouble sleeping or sleep too much, experience changes in appetite, or have thoughts about death or suicide, you need to get help from a professional. Problems can be emotional or they can be related to hormonal or other physical changes. Your health is important. Take care of you!

WEEK ONE

THE ME I WANT TO BE

Answer a few questions about your feelings. Then take time to reflect on who you are and who you want to be. There is plenty of time for you to become the you who has always been waiting inside! This is the best time of your life. Take advantage of the endless opportunities of being you.

The thing I like best about the way I look is: _____

_____

_____

_____

People like to talk to me because: _____

_____

_____

_____

The best idea I ever had was: _____

_____

_____

_____

The most fun I ever had was when: _____

_____

_____

_____

The biggest risk I ever took was: _____

_____

_____

_____

My core belief or philosophy of life is: _____

_____

_____

_____

The one thing I would most like to change about myself is: _____

_____

_____

_____

The one thing about me that I would most like to pass along to my grandchild is:

_____

_____

_____

_____

WEEK TWO

ME AND NOT ME

It is not until halfway through the second year of life that infants learn to recognize their own image and to coordinate the image they see in a mirror with the action of touching their body. Psychologist William James in 1890 observed that one of the giant tasks of infancy is to accomplish "one great splitting of the whole universe into two halves...we call the two halves 'me' and 'not me'." If your grandchild is under 18 months of age, she will not have a fully developed sense of self. However, even at a very early age, you can begin to help your grandchild develop positive feelings about the "me" she will come to know.

You may enjoy filling in dates and describing actions that let you know that your grandchild is developing a sense of self. Look for these markers along the trail to self-esteem.

Event	Age	Date	Describe Action
Cries for a particular person	_____	_____	_____
Responds to his name	_____	_____	_____
Shows shyness with strangers	_____	_____	_____
Pats image of self in mirror	_____	_____	_____
Drinks from a cup	_____	_____	_____
Feeds self	_____	_____	_____
Takes off shoes	_____	_____	_____
Kisses pictures	_____	_____	_____
Responds selectively to others	_____	_____	_____
Distinguishes "me" and "you"	_____	_____	_____
Identifies body parts	_____	_____	_____
Touches own body while looking at image of self in mirror	_____	_____	_____
Shows awareness of gender – self or other (aware of being boy or girl)	_____	_____	_____

Watching your grandchild become a "real person" is fun.
Be positive. Be involved. Be yourself.

WEEK THREE

THE REAL WORLD AND SELF-ESTEEM

Sociologist G. David Johnson coined the term "social dyslexia" to describe the apparent malady of some people who seem to read in reverse all the cues given to them about their behavior. As a college professor, I have often faced a student who has just asked me the question, "Do I need to come to class for all of your lectures?" My reply is usually, "That is up to you. I think your decision should have a lot to do with the grade you wish to make." Perhaps there is not as much evidence of my opinion in my sarcastic tone as is needed, but each quarter some students make the choice to stay away from class although they hear me tell them in so many words that their grade will suffer for poor attendance.

I believe that it is the moral responsibility of adults to help children to interpret the cues that people give them about themselves. This is actually a rather radical idea in the worlds of education and child development. The more conventional concept is that adults should praise children lavishly and in so doing raise their self-esteem and self-confidence. I think we have carried that notion to the point of harming our children and our society. Evidence from research on juvenile crime and delinquency reveals that juvenile offenders often have very high self-esteem. Indeed, they think there are no barriers to their doing whatever they want to do. Gangs are a great source of praise, but for what? Teachers, eager to compensate for their students' family and neighborhood environments, sometimes offer good grades and other rewards for mediocre work.

I recently finished a research project on the career aspirations of neglected and delinquent youth. When asked what jobs they expected to have when they finished high school, the most prevalent responses from adolescents who were living in group homes or who were in detention centers for juvenile offenders were jobs such as sports star, popular music idol, or movie star. I find that very sad because there is more going on there than a child simply expressing high hopes. These adolescents have unrealistic expectations that will keep them from working on skills that would serve them well in competing for the jobs that are really available to them. A 15-year-old with a drug abuse problem and three months left to spend in a detention center needs to know that a modest talent on the neighborhood basketball court will not catapult him out of his world of poverty and drugs. Praise him for what he does well, but remind him that a good education and appropriate therapy for his addiction will make his life better. However, few people get that one-in-a-million chance at stardom.

On the other hand, it is important that the adults in a child's life learn to watch for and accept exceptional talent when it appears. Annie presented to her second-grade teacher a picture of a forest in which she had drawn each tree with carefully executed branches and leaves. The trees in her drawing stood in stark contrast to the typical ball-topped straight trunks of trees drawn by most second graders. Annie half-chuckles and half-cries as she remembers her disappointment over the teacher's reaction to her drawing – "You can't even draw a tree." Somehow, Annie's belief in herself helped her to overcome the teacher's evaluation. Annie's artistic ability has been confirmed many times during her 25-year career as a master artist for a major publishing house and art director for a large manufacturing company. Helping a child to develop a realistic self-image means being able as adults to accept what is really good as well as to steer the child toward career and personal goals that are well-matched to her abilities and resources. We must be aware of our own motivations in evaluating a child's talents.

Often, we foster in our children unrealistic expectations because we feel so disappointed that we let go our own fantastic dreams. When I was a miserable 8th grader, and who isn't, I sat in algebra class and dreamed about the day I would marry a member of the Diplomatic Corps and move to some exotic place where housekeepers were affordable and there was an occasion for a ball gown every night. I remember my parents telling me that their greatest hope for me was that I would someday be happily married – but just in case that did not happen, they were planning to pay for my college education. Oh, I never really lost the dream. Why, just the other day I was fantasizing that someone cleaned my house for under $75. But most of my dreams that have come true have been directly linked to the education my parents gave me and the sense of self they helped me to develop. Thanks, Mom & Dad!

Try this exercise to help base your grandchild's expectations in the real world.

1. List here all of the famous people you know. Do not include those you have paid for a ticket to see. By "know" I mean that you have had at least one conversation in which they called you by your name.

_____   _____

_____   _____

_____   _____

_____   _____

2. List here all the everyday people whom you consider to be heroic, important, or worthy of being imitated by your grandchild. Write a brief statement of your reason for admiring each one. Save this list and talk about it with your grandchild when he is old enough.

_____

_____

_____

_____

_____

_____

_____

_____

3. What do you think it takes to make a person a hero?

_____

_____

_____

_____

The world is full of real-life heroes. Introduce your grandchild to the wonderful people around her. Give your grandchild the hope that is in attainable dreams.

WEEK FOUR

LOVE'S IMAGE:
HOW MEN AND WOMEN GOT LABELED AS LOVE'S POLAR OPPOSITES

I cannot leave a discussion on self-image and self-esteem without taking note of one aspect of self-image as it relates to gender, specifically, the polarization of men and women in matters of the heart. For the life of me, I do not know where we got the idea in our society that women have all the feelings and men are cold as stone. Sometimes I wonder if I grew up on another planet – or did I dream that my father kissed his grown sons or cried when my dog died? Doesn't anyone else have a warm, fuzzy, teddy bear brother? If men are so heartless, why are there flower shops or lingerie catalogues? Dr. John Gray has explained the different approaches of men and women to love by telling us that men are from Mars and women are from Venus, metaphorically of course. But I'll take Shakespeare's side on this one and suggest that "The fault, dear Brutus, is not in our stars, but in ourselves." Those of us who believe that men and women are by nature or accident of birth polar opposites where love and sensitivity are concerned have swallowed society's line.

The differences in men and women in the areas of love and sensitivity are direct results of their socialization experiences. Little boys grow up to be insensitive and to hide their emotions if they grow up in a household and community where such behavior is expected and rewarded. Psychologists Carol Gilligan and Nancy Chodorow have given evidence in their writings that women are better at love and intimacy because they are better at building connections. That is a skill, not a character trait! I don't know who was the first woman who told her young son to keep a stiff upper lip when he wanted to cry over his skinned knee, but I do know that for that moment, she forgot that one day he would be a husband. She forgot that crying over pain is a natural emotional response. She forgot her own feelings of need for companionship and understanding from her husband and she started to raise her son to be insensitive.

Earlier in this chapter, we talked about the self-image as a reflection in the mirror of perceptions of us that other people have. I suggest that men would not have decided that it was acceptable for them to be insensitive if they had not been rewarded by their mothers, wives, and the rest of society for being so. Women would not have become love's poster children if they had not been rewarded for their softness, intuition, caring, and tenderness. Anyone except the most dysfunctional among us is capable of love. What we need is mothers and grandmothers who remember that they are raising the boys in their family to be the men who will respond to some woman's needs. We need fathers and grandfathers who are brave enough to watch their sons and grandsons cry and laugh and feel real life. Similarly, we need to allow our daughters to be achievers, to be strong and independent when that behavior is appropriate to the situation. To do less than to allow our children of either gender to experience their full range of emotional capabilities is to impose on them the crippling gender stereotypes of our past.

This next exercise will help you to think about your own gender self-image and the goals that you have for yourself and your grandchild in the realm of love and emotion. Think about your own needs and who has met them. Think about the stereotypes that you may have about men, women, and love. Think about who you are and who you want to be as a giver of love and affection. Think about your grandchild's future as a person who will give and get love.

This exercise will help you to link your expectations for adult gender self-images with your feelings about your young grandchild. I think we often forget that the person who will be an adult is the same person who is now that beloved adorable infant or toddler who fills our lives with so much pleasure. What if you could help your grandchild, boy or girl, keep that open spirit that is so ready to express love? Well, that is no fantasy. You can. Try this exercise to see how you feel about your grandchild's emotions and how he expresses them.

1. Find a picture of your grandchild smiling. As you look at the picture, say each of the following statements. Be firm. Say them as if you mean them.

   (A) Don't do that. Only sissies smile!
   (B) That's it, sweetheart. Give Gran a big smile!

Which of those statements made you feel better? _____

2. Find a picture of your grandchild crying. As you look at the picture, say each of the following statements. Be firm. Say them as if you mean them.

   (A) Don't do that. Only sissies cry!
   (B) That's it, sweetheart. If you feel like crying, go ahead and cry!

Which of those statements made you feel better? _____

3. Find a picture of your grandchild doing something that you think is funny. As you look at the picture, say each of the following statements. Be firm. Say them as if you mean them.

   (A) Don't do that. Who do you think you are, Groucho Marx?
   (B) That's it, sweetheart. See how you make Gran laugh!

Which of those statements made you feel better?_____

Don't you feel better when you let your grandchild be who he is? Doesn't it feel right to allow her to express the emotions that she feels? Whether your grandchild is a girl or boy makes little difference in the feeling you get when he shows you his heart.

My point is that emotions are your grandchild's soul showing through. To stifle that process now is to change forever her ability to connect to other people in relationships. You can help your grandchild to have healthy and happy and loving relationships throughout his lifetime by helping him to discover and express the emotions that are inside him. Of course, there is a bonus waiting for you as well. You get to know all the wonderful feelings that make your grandchild who he is. In teaching him skills to connect with others, you are strengthening for yourself the connection between you and your grandchild. Enjoy!

MY FAVORITE PICTURE OF ME

Date: _____   Place: _____

MY FAVORITE PICTURE OF MY GRANDCHILD

Date: _____   Place: _____

CHAPTER 9

※

SHARING WITH GRANDCHILDREN THE VALUE OF WORK

Sara was born into a dual career family. Simply put, that means that her mother and her father both have careers that are important to them. Beyond that, her grandmothers and grandfathers on both sides are still working in careers that they enjoy. There is only one household on Sara's street in which there is a stay-at-home mom, and she is home schooling her children, which keeps her as busy as would a full-time teaching job in a neighborhood school. Jason was born to a single mom who works full time and takes classes at a community college near their apartment. Jason's dad and his paternal grandparents are not really part of his life. His maternal grandmother lives with Jason and his mom. She works full time at a day care center and struggles to provide for the needs of her 80-year-old mother who has arthritis. These are the children of today's families. Work is an important aspect of life and its impact on children is considerable in modern American society.

In this chapter, we will explore what work means in your life. We will examine ways in which your work may have an impact on your child-rearing practices and your goals for your grandchild's education and career. We will also look at how adults influence the attitudes that children have about their later career choices. Then we will explore some ways that businesses can help families to resolve conflicts between their dependent care responsibilities and the demands of their work.

Sociologists have shown us that parents from different work backgrounds have different child-rearing practices. For example, a father who works for a large corporation may try to help his child to develop skills in negotiating and getting along with others, while a nurse may want her children to develop accuracy and diligence in finishing tasks. We bring expectations from our workplaces into our homes and family lives. Many of us find our jobs to be a source of friendships as well as income. The workplace can be an important contributor to our self-image. We want our children and grandchildren to be successful and so we teach them the skills that we think have served us well.

One thing on which parents from most occupational backgrounds and most employers agree is that the workforce of tomorrow needs to consist of responsible workers. Employers want people who can be trusted to carry their own weight and to complete work assignments. Quality is the key to success in a competitive world market. Businesses want to employ people who take responsibility for the work that they do or the products they help to produce. You can help your grandchild to become a responsible worker by fostering in her responsibility within the family environment. Here are some suggestions about building responsibility in your grandchild's character.

TIPS ON HOW TO HELP YOUR GRANDCHILD BECOME RESPONSIBLE (adapted from a list compiled by Nancy Jones, Child Development Specialist)
Responsible adults – parents and grandparents – have responsible children.
Be a responsible role model.
Give the child responsibilities that are appropriate for her age and skill level.
Praise reinforces responsible behavior. Nagging causes delay and leads to irresponsible behavior.
Young children need cues, reminders that prompt responses. Providing cues is not the same as nagging. Help the child to remember. Don't do the work of remembering for him.
Assume that the child wants to be responsible. Allow her to make choices rather than to have you make assignments.
Allow the child to see that his efforts make a difference. Cooperation comes when the problem is understood and the results of efforts to solve it are tangible.
Allow the child to suffer the consequences of her own behavior. Of course, do not put the child at risk for harm, but let her learn that failure to behave responsibly can produce undesirable results. For example, do not replace a toy that is ruined when left outside in the rain.
A positive self-image aids responsibility. Children who believe in their own competence are willing to accept responsibility. Help your grandchild to know when he does something well.
Show your confidence in your grandchild. Positive expectations from adults guide children toward more responsible behavior.
Everyone shirks responsibility from time to time. Give a second chance without reprimand. What you want to avoid is a pattern of irresponsible behavior.

You can also foster responsibility in your grandchild by taking a more democratic approach to decision making about everyday life. For example, if your grandchild visits frequently and leaves toys scattered all over your house, you can include him in the decision about how to handle the problem. "Meet" with him and other family members. Let the group choose the best course of action. Then expect your grandchild and all other decision makers to follow the "rules" that were set by the group. Let your grandchild see you praise those who accomplish the tasks that were determined by the group. Perhaps Pop-Pop's task is to pick up toys in the living room and your grandchild is assigned to pick up toys in the bedroom. Call another meeting after a trial period. Talk about how your plan of action is working. Listen to your grandchild's ideas and let him hear your praise and/or complaints. Participation in family decision making gives your grandchild the experience and the confidence to behave responsibly in other settings.

Your life has great influence on your grandchild in so many ways. Your educational background and work experience provide a context for the educational and job aspirations of your children and grandchildren. If you dislike your job, you may encourage younger members of your family to get more education so they can get a better job or to emphasize a different educational track than yours so they will have a different career path. If you are happy with your job, the children in your family will notice your job satisfaction and they will have a positive view of the work that you do and its value to the family.

There has been a lot of discussion about the impact of a mother's career on her family life. Since men were traditionally the ones who left home to work, many people have worried that the increase in women's employment outside the home would have a detrimental effect on their children. Whether a mother's employment will have positive or negative impact on her daughter's school achievement and career choices seems to be directly related to the mother's attitudes about her work. Sociologist Greer Litton Fox has done research on daughters whose mothers work full time. She has found high achievement in school and positive attitudes about work among daughters when their mothers are satisfied with their jobs. Of course, work satisfaction for a woman is linked to her feelings about the support she gets at home. If other family members provide emotional support and assistance with household tasks, the working woman is likely to be more satisfied with her life in general and her work in particular. Feelings about work and family are connected.

Sometimes the influence of work on family life is not positive. Research has shown that stress on the job can make workers generally unhappy with their lives and that unhappiness can spill over into family relationships. Employers have become aware in recent years of the importance of happy home lives in making workers more productive. Employee assistance programs are offered as part of the benefits packages in many companies. Various educational and counseling programs help workers to address personal and family problems and to manage work-related stress. Many companies also encourage their workers to become more aware of personal health, fitness, and safety for themselves and their families. If you are a working grandparent, you are many things to many people. Stop occasionally and examine your priorities. As you move into new phases of your life, you may find that money is less valuable than is the time to be all that you want to be in your family and community environments. If you want to continue to work, investigate to see if your employer offers programs that can help you to manage the stress that can come from juggling your many roles.

Perhaps the most significant change that has occurred in American family life from the period of your childhood to this time in which your grandchild will spend his growing years is the dramatic increase in the numbers of women with children who are employed full time. Women are delaying marriage and child bearing, but even with adjustments in the timing of these life transitions, 59% of white women with infants and 64% of African American women with infants are working full time and over 60% of mothers with children under school age have full time jobs.

At the other end of the life span, older people who need care are not finding it as readily available from women as in the past. While the trend in recent years has been for men to retire at younger ages, women are working longer than before. Many women aged 55-64, the prime ages for needing to care for frail older parents, are employed full time and simply cannot afford to or do not want to give up their jobs to care for elderly family members. Substitute sources of care have to be found or these women must take on caregiving tasks in addition to their work. Men are increasingly involved in elder care as well as child care, but over 75% of the family care given to elders is still provided by wives, daughters, and daughters-in-law.

With so many women in the work force, employers have felt pressure to respond to family needs for child care and elder care. The Family Leave Act of 1993 assured men and women that they would not lose their jobs if they took time off to care for their close relatives, but this legislation provided no compensation for providing care. Companies are reporting that both men and women are taking advantage of the benefits assured by this legislation. AT&T, which employs approximately 135,000 workers, had a 400 to 1 ratio of women to men taking advantage of family leave in the first year after passage of the Family Leave Act. Last year, the ratio was 18 women to 1 man. Not only is the legislation giving women the help they need in balancing work duties and family care responsibilities, but it seems to be creating more equality in the distribution of family care responsibility among mothers and fathers and sons and daughters. There is one problem that was not addressed in the Family Leave Act. No one seems to have figured out so far how such legislation can guarantee that the absent worker will not lose ground in a competitive job market while fulfilling family care responsibilities. Workers, particularly women, are still afraid of being labeled as caregivers and put on "the mommy track" or "the caregiving daughter track."

Child and elder care can be costly to family members and to businesses that lose good workers. For example, approximately 10% of working caregivers quit their jobs in order to provide full time care for a dependent elderly family member. Businesses must train replacements. Expertise is lost, usually in the prime of someone's work life. The losses that can result from work and child care conflicts are even more serious, in my opinion. Rather than lose income or career status, families sometimes decide to resolve their child care problems by parenting on "split shifts." That is, one parent will work days and the other will work evenings. While this arrangement provides full time parental coverage of child care, it means that parents rarely spend time together and that the child rarely has the opportunity to interact with the family as a unit. How can a family build an "us" when they spend little time together in the same place? Sociologist Harriet Presser's research has shown that marriages are less stable in families where partners work nonstandard hours. If the primary caregivers for your grandchild have chosen split-shift parenting as a solution to work and family conflicts, then your family will need to take special care to be sure that your grandchild has time to see his parents together and to experience their joint care. It takes a lot of effort for working parents and grandparents to build a family "us," but the results are well worth it!

There is another kind of cooperation necessary to produce happy, healthy, supported children in a society that places so much emphasis on the work of adults outside their homes. That is the cooperation of businesses and families. Family care in our time requires the concerted efforts of businesses, community resources, and family members. Within the family, the demands of work and the responsibilities of family care can produce conflict. The entire family will benefit if the family treats care of its dependent members as a family matter, approaching child and elder care responsibilities from the base of a family "us." But families cannot do it alone. Families increasingly depend on business and community help with care for the young and the old. Businesses can help by being flexible in structuring jobs. Job sharing, flexible job scheduling, and working at home can provide child and elder care solutions. On-site care centers and care referral services can also help families to resolve conflicts between work and family care responsibilities. Community-based solutions to work and family conflicts include child and adult day care centers, after school care programs, and in-home care services.

Some businesses have been at the forefront of the effort to solve work and family conflicts for more than a decade. I spent four years as chairperson of the Work and Family Focus Group of the National Council on Family Relations. During that time, I co-edited with Dr. Marvin Sussman a book on *Corporations, Businesses, and Families.* Both of those experiences made me keenly aware of the commitment of some corporations to the family lives of their own employees and to the benefits to our society that will result from strengthening the families of the current and future work force. This book that you are reading is the result of such commitment. The Warren-Featherbone Company and Mercantile Stores launched the Connecting the Generations project because their leaders were aware that grandparents of the new millennium are vital to their families and our society. The Connecting the Generations Project is a crusade of support by business for American families of the 21st century.

I want to call your attention to some other exemplary efforts by businesses to meet the needs of families in their work organizations and in our communities. You and your family are not alone.

In 1992, 137 organizations joined together to invest $25.4 million for dependent child and elder care. Leaders in that project were such familiar corporate names as Allstate Insurance, American Express, Amoco, AT&T, Eastman Kodak, Exxon, IBM, Johnson & Johnson, Motorola, The Travelers, and Xerox. Describing the initiative, the CEOs released this statement, "We can accomplish more by working together than by working alone. We must attract and retain a productive and motivated workforce and help them realize their full potential if our businesses are to be competitive now and in the future. [A primary goal of this effort] is to increase the supply and enhance the quality of a broad range of dependent care programs. These programs respond to the diverse needs of families, particularly those with infants and children in school – our next generation of employees." Three years later, more corporations, such as Citibank, Hewlett Packard, NYNEX, and Texaco joined the project and an additional $100 million was invested to fund over 1,000 dependent care projects. Harvard Business School Professor Rosabeth Moss Kanter said, "This strong investment in families by so many leading companies sends a powerful message about the commitment American businesses are willing to make to their employees even at a time of traumatic downsizing." (Wanger Associates, 1992 & 1995)

DuPont, a chemical and energy company, has conducted extensive research on work and family issues and now has a decade of data to share with other businesses and families. Among the findings reported by DuPont are these. Employees have fewer concerns about their dependent child and elder care arrangements than they did 10 years ago. Business initiatives and resource and referral services have helped. Employees with elder care responsibilities and those of the "sandwich generation" who have both elder care and child care responsibilities report the most stress and highest burnout. Elder care is also more expensive on average than child care. Employees who provide elder care for their relatives say that they spend $2,000-$10,000 per year of their own money, in addition to using resources of the elder family member or public sources of support. Among DuPont's work/family initiatives are: "Just in Time Care" – a program that links employees to backup and emergency dependent care and subsidizes the cost at 80%; "Life/Works Family Resource Program" – a toll-free service that provides consultation and referrals and is currently used by 20% of DuPont's employees; flexible work schedules and places; and dependent care reimbursement for business travel.

Working Mother magazine ranks corporations and gives an annual award to the 100 Best Companies for Working Mothers. The companies are evaluated on wages, opportunities for women to advance, support for child care, flexibility (work schedules and workplace), and family friendly benefits (family leave policy, resource and referral services, dependent care). The award program is important because it helps to give those companies a competitive edge in attracting desirable employees and it gives visibility to corporations that are good citizens of our communities. You can encourage your local media and civic groups to recognize those businesses in your community that support working parents and grandparents.

Many business based projects that assist families have grown from ideas that were suggested by employees who realized that other families must have needs similar to their own. Here are some good resources that you may use if you want to find out more about what businesses can do to support families or if you want to make suggestions to your employer:

Work & Family Connection
5197 Beachside Drive
Minnetanka, MN 55343
1-800-487-7898
e-mail: Info@workfamily.com
Consulting, $245 annual membership fee for newsletter
and database search privileges

Work/Family Directions
930 Commonwealth Ave.
Boston, MA 02215-1212
1-617-278-4000
http://www.wfd.com
Consulting, research, resource and referral services in the
U.S., Canada, and the U.K.

The first exercise in this chapter is designed to help you recognize your own attitudes about work and family. The choices that you made for your education and career came out of the context of your family's work history and your perception of what your family expected of you. Those career choices have influenced your child rearing goals and practices. Now that you have grandchildren, you may have expectations about what careers they will choose. You may also have strong opinions about how your children should balance their career and family lives. Take some time to examine your feelings about work and family by completing the first exercise.

WEEK ONE

A TALE OF TWO WORLDS:
FAMILY EXPECTATIONS ABOUT WORK

Fill in this chart. Think about your feelings about your own work and family lives. How did you fare at fulfilling expectations that others had for you or that you had for yourself?

	What my parents wanted or expected	What I wanted	What really happened
My Jobs/Career			
My Family Life			
My Children's Jobs/Careers			
My Children's Family Lives			

How did you feel about your parents' expectations for you? _____

_____

_____

_____

How do you suppose your children and grandchildren feel about knowing that you have certain expectations for them? (You might want to ask them.)

_____

_____

_____

_____

WEEK TWO

"A Rose By Any Other Name" Might Still Be An Engineer

This second exercise will help you to see how your own educational and career aspirations can influence your grandchildren's choices. Probably the most important way in which you can influence your grandchild's work life is to expose her to a variety of experiences that will help her to know what are her talents and interests. In addition to what you do for your grandchild, you can become part of a family "us." You can support the work and child rearing efforts of your children as they parent your grandchildren.

My children's grandfather gave his son a name that he thought would "sound good with Dr. in front of it." As it turned out, little Bobby grew up to be an engineer and economist and the only "Dr." in the family was a daughter-in-law with a Ph.D. There is little scientific evidence that giving your child or grandchild a particular name has any influence on her career choice, but there is considerable evidence that providing positive experiences in math or science can turn the little tyke's interests in that direction or that giving a child violin lessons can increase his chances of choosing a career as a musician.

Do you have career aspirations for your grandchild? Have there been four generations of lawyers in your family and do you want your grandchild to continue the tradition? Are you impressed with the benefits of a military career and are you now hoping that your grandchild will choose that path? As you complete this exercise, think about how you might influence your grandchild's career choices. Remember that children and adolescents may respond better to subtle guidance toward a career than to threats or bribes such as, "I will only pay for your education if you go to medical school." If you want your grandchild to be a physician, start early by turning visits to the pediatrician into fun and educational outings. Later, encourage your grandchild in math and science studies, but do not neglect the social sciences and humanities. Medical school admission boards are now looking favorably on applications from candidates who have well-rounded educational backgrounds.

This "game" is played with blocks – wooden or plastic will do. Place one block on a flat surface in front of you. Each time you answer a question, add a block to your stack. Soon, you will see how your influence on your grandchild can build. Don't worry if your block stack collapses – just start over with some new and even more creative ways to make your mark in your grandchild's work life.

The first four building blocks are appropriate for a grandchild of any age. The last two blocks give you something to think about now and to arrange when your grandchild is older. As you stack the blocks, take time to think about your influence on your grandchild. Think about ways to encourage him to make choices that are best for him.

BLOCK #1 What talents and skills in my grandchild have I observed that might contribute to a successful career choice?

_____

_____

_____

_____

BLOCK #2 What careers have I heard my grandchild express an interest in? (For a young child this might be as simple as the child pointing to a policeman or having a good relationship with a teacher or day care worker.)

_____

_____

_____

_____

BLOCK #3 What games and toys can I give him that will develop talents and skills that he or she has?

_____

_____

_____

_____

BLOCK #4 What activities and educational experiences can I encourage my grandchild to participate in that would prepare him or her for a successful career?

_____

_____

_____

_____

BLOCK #5 Who do I know in the community, who is happy in his or her career, that might let my grandchild visit for an hour or two?

_____

_____

_____

_____

BLOCK #6 Is there an internship or part-time job that I might arrange for my grandchild which might help him or her to make a wise career decision?

_____

_____

_____

_____

WEEK THREE

"I Can't Babysit. I'm Working."

Whether you are a working grandparent or you are retired, you have a life! If there is one characteristic that sets today's grandparents apart from the grandparents of generations past, it is their level of activity and involvement with the world outside their families. Volunteer work, educational opportunities, travel, and careers pull young and vibrant grandparents in many directions – none of which leave much time for baby sitting. This exercise is designed to help you look at your time priorities where your grandchildren are concerned. Remember as you complete this exercise that **IT IS OK TO BE YOU!** It is better to honestly face your limitations on traditional grandparenting activities than to allow your children and grandchildren to develop unrealistic expectations about your availability.

Rank the following by writing a number in the blank beside each category/activity. **Use the number 1 for your highest priority**. First rank the category headings and then go back and rank the activities within each category. When the exercise is completed, you will have ranked the categories (1-4) and the activities in each category (1-5).

Working at my job or volunteer activity: _____

    Spending the required time   _____
    Doing extra work that requires more time   _____
    Participating in work related clubs or organizations   _____
    Taking work related classes   _____
    Other work related activities   _____

Taking care of myself physically and mentally: _____

    Learning more about my health   _____
    Visiting a doctor, mental health counselor, or therapist   _____
    Going to a gym or participating in a regular exercise program   _____
    Doing something fun, a recreational activity   _____
    Other physical or mental health activities   _____

Taking care of my spiritual needs: _____

    Participating in religious activities   _____
    Reading or meditating   _____
    Spending time with someone who understands my soul   _____
    Doing something good for other people   _____
    Other spiritual activities   _____

Spending time with my grandchild: _____

    Babysitting while my grandchildren's parents work or "play"   _____
    Having my grandchild in my home for a visit   _____
    Taking my grandchild on an outing (educational or fun)   _____
    Volunteering in my grandchild's school or day care center   _____
    Other activities with my grandchild   _____

WEEK FOUR

WORK/FAMILY/COMMUNITY CONNECTIONS

This exercise will help you to see that your family is not alone in its need to balance work and family priorities. Whether or not you think you will ever use the services, take the time to list what is available in your community. The list may be impressive. If there are gaps that you recognize, you may be able to influence business and community leaders to implement needed programs.

List three businesses in your community that have family-friendly programs such as on-site day care, resource and referral services for dependent care, flextime or flexplace work arrangements.

#1 _____
#2 _____
#3 _____

List three social service agencies in your community that help working parents or grandparents to resolve work/family conflicts.

#1 _____
#2 _____
#3 _____

List three services that are needed but do not exist in your community to help working parents or grandparents to resolve work/family conflicts.

#1 _____
#2 _____
#3 _____

List three things that you will do to make a difference in your community or in your family regarding work/family issues.

#1 _____
#2 _____
#3 _____

You can make things better for your family and for other families in your community. You can build a family "us" and you can work to make businesses in your area aware of the needs of working caregivers. It is all a matter of building connections.

REFLECTIONS ON WORK AND FAMILY

_____

_____

_____

_____

_____

_____

_____

_____

_____

_____

_____

_____

CHAPTER 10

YOU'VE GOT A FRIEND

Winter, spring, summer, or fall
All you've got to do is call,
And I'll be there, yes I will.
You've got a friend.

                                   – James Taylor

"I want him to know that I'll always be there for him." That is what grandparents told the Connecting the Generations team when we conducted focus groups to find out what was important to grandparents of the new millennium. Later, we conducted a survey of grandparents which drew over 170 responses. Once again, grandparents told us, "I want to give love and to offer a safe, secure atmosphere, a place that is always there."

The security that you provide for your grandchild when he is an infant becomes the foundation for trust in childhood and confidence when he becomes a young adult. One grandmother who answered our survey included in her reply the text of a card that her 19-year-old grandson wrote on her 70th birthday.

> You have impacted my life so greatly. You have been more than a grandmother to me. You are my friend, my mentor, and my confidante. You said you had a lot riding on this horse. Well, he realizes it and is going to be the best he can possibly be to make good on your faith. You have shown me how to turn adversity into advantage. We're a great team.

Connecting the Generations is for grandparents who want what this grandmother got for her birthday. This book, all the research and planning that has been done by the Connecting the Generations team, and all the efforts that you have put into being an active and soulful grandparent are all about building the kind of relationship which this young man has with his grandmother. And guess what – you can do it!

Remember, you and your grandchild are growing together. As you develop the connection between your soul and your grandchild's, both of you are learning how to reach deeply inside your spirits and to pull out the words and actions that create trust, confidence, security, and love. You may think of the process as being your contribution to your grandchild's development, but there is more. If you become that "place that is always there" for your grandchild, then you will have a place where you can always go as well. If your grandchild gets a confidante, so do you. Oh, you may not talk to each other about exactly the same things. It is probably not a good idea to pour your adult problems onto your grandchild's young head, but you can without harming her enjoy the comfort and security of knowing that someone in this world will always want to listen to you and will always want what is best for you. Love and trust flow in both directions.

Research on human social psychological development has shown that we really do not need a great number of close relationships in our lives. In fact, a single confidante seems to be enough to make a significant difference between good or poor health for a person in later life. Oh, of course we may enjoy a variety of activities and the people that go along with them. Diversity in our friendships helps to keep life interesting. But everyone needs at least one person in whom we can confide and by whom we feel loved and supported unconditionally.

Did you know that research has shown that married men live longer and healthier lives than unmarried men? But there does not seem to be a similar effect among women. Hold on – before you women start making your list of all the reasons that fact does not surprise you – think about the differences in men and women in their relationships with spouses and with friends. Women have a wider range of friends and they confide in more people than do men. A happily married man is very likely to report that his wife is his best friend. Women, on the other hand, may have a group of "best friends" and may even confide in their friendship groups things that they would never share with their husbands. It is easy to see then why marriage is more critical to a man's health and well being than to a woman's. He may have put all his eggs in one basket – his spouse. She probably has maintained more varied sources of social support.

Grandmothers may find it easier to think about being a friend and confidante for their grandchild than will grandfathers. There is no innate difference in the love that grandmothers and grandfathers have for their grandchildren, but there are differences in the ways that men and women establish and maintain intimacy and confidential relationships. This does not preclude grandfathers and grandchildren from having exceptionally strong bonds. It means only that grandfathers may have to work a bit to modify their thinking about family relationships. Men tend to relate by role. That is, men are more likely to treat family members in ways that are prescribed by who they are rather than how they feel about them. A grandfather may have notions about how a grandson or granddaughter is supposed to be treated. He may need to get around feelings about prescribed roles in order to see the friendship that waits for him in his grandson or granddaughter. In contrast, a grandmother may react more from her emotions in forming relationships with her grandchildren. If so, she may find it easier to relate to them as friends and confidantes.

There is a delicate balance that must be maintained in friendships between grandparents and grandchildren. Family relationships come in layers and those layers are necessary. While grandparents and grandchildren may rely upon each other for emotional support and may become friends and confidantes, children do not understand adults who abandon their authoritative roles and try to act as peers to the children. Especially in adolescence, young people are confused by adults who want to relate to them as peers. When the whole world, including her own body, is changing around your grandchild, she needs to be able to predict that her grandfather will act within a range of behaviors that she understands as appropriate for an adult. Toddlers have similar needs and expectations. You may sit on the floor and play a game or put together a puzzle at eye level with your grandchild, but when he decides to throw a toy at his baby sister, you need to be able to intervene as an adult.

A potentially negative aspect of grandparent/grandchild friendships is that the child's parents may feel threatened by your being her confidante. Indeed, it is easy to turn close relationships between grandparents and grandchildren into conspiracies against parental authority. But wary grandparents can enjoy the benefits of a great relationship with their grandchildren without undermining the decisions of parents. You can be your grandchild's sounding board. Let him try out ideas on you, talk things out with you, and share excitement and disappointment with you. In short, be who you are, be interested in what your grandchild has to say, and be aware that raising a child is a family matter. Children need to understand that all of the adults around them have their best interests at heart. They need to see a family "us" in which parents and grandparents work together for the good of the children and for the whole family.

You know, in the history of our society, there were not always such dividing lines between the generations. When we were an agricultural society, less concentrated in cities with homes less distant from places of work, the generational relationships in our families were also different. For one thing, the childbearing years represented a greater percentage of the years of a woman's adult life. Consequently, there were more children born into our families and a wider range of age from the oldest to the youngest. There were also greater age gaps between men and women who were married to each other. Young women frequently died in childbirth and men were married two or three times, still to young women, in order to have more children. The results were families in which a wife might be very near the same age of the older siblings and a husband might be near the same age of some of the grandparents. This blurring of generational lines created some interesting family relationships. Slowly, our families evolved into the structures that we know today – parents very close to each other in age, siblings born within 2-5 years of each other, and grandparents set apart by age and living arrangements.

At the same time that changes were occurring in the organization of families by age, trends were developing outside the family that created generational differences in our families and in our society as a whole. Among the most significant changes, historian Howard Chudacoff has listed:

- age-grading in schools;
- the "discovery" of life stages, most importantly adolescence and old age, by psychologists and sociologists;
- recognition of age differences under the law, particularly child labor laws; *and*
- the rise of an age-graded popular culture, including age differences in preferences for music.

These influences outside the family punctuated our beliefs that children, parents, and grandparents had not only different roles, but also gulfs between them in regard to likes and dislikes and needs. We more or less threw out the baby with the bath water when it came to our expectations about close and emotionally supportive relationships between family members of different generations. Grandparents today are challenging these notions that are based on generational differences. We are looking across generational lines for similarities in interests and experiences, while maintaining family roles that help our children and grandchildren develop a sense of order and appropriateness in family relationships.

Once again, generational lines are blurring. Visit a college campus near you. Look into a classroom full of students. Count the gray heads and obviously middle-aged body types. No longer are college classrooms filled with 20-year-olds. Higher education is appropriate for everyone. By the way, that can work in reverse as well. A couple of years ago an exceptionally bright 10-year-old received his degree from the institution where I teach.

Further, today's grandparents do not always "act their age." We now recognize a whole new age category, the "young old,"of 55-75 year olds who are healthy and active. Retirement is no longer a period of inactivity and well-deserved rest that immediately precedes death, rather a period of renewal and creativity in trying new adventures. Where interests are concerned, you may have a lot in common with your grandchildren. Research has shown many similarities in interests among teens and the young-old. Guess what two age groups are the champion shoppers in our society. That's right – adolescents and 55-64 year olds are the lifeblood of the retail industry. From using computers for fun, to dating, to getting an education, to recreational shopping, adolescents and mid-lifers are out there together storming the Internet, malls, techno-stores, coffee shops, and community colleges.

Unfortunately, the problem of childhood sexual abuse of American children has had an impact on relationships between grandparents and grandchildren. Adults are generally more cautious about touching children and being alone with children since reports of sexual abuse of children have increased. It is difficult to determine how prevalent is sexual abuse of children within their families. Adults are reluctant to believe a child who accuses an adult in the family and adults often hope that the problem will go away if they ignore it. Taking into account the under reporting, research indicates that childhood sexual abuse occurs in 15-20% of American families. Grandparents are rarely the perpetrators. In fact, 90% of the abusers are fathers or stepfathers. Almost half of the abusers suffered abuse themselves when they were children. Whenever it occurs, childhood sexual abuse in families is likely to leave scars that last for generations to come. One of the saddest effects of this blight on American family life is that it has added to our fears of intimacy, leaving adults in families afraid to show the physical affection that children need. Grandparents can be effective advocates for children. You may want to get involved with abuse prevention organizations in your community. We can stop childhood sexual abuse in our time if we make it a priority. We can make it safe for all of our families to be the intimate havens that our children need and want.

I know that some of you are separated from your precious grandchildren either because they live far from you or because there is tension in your relationships with one or both of their parents. It is difficult to love someone who is not accessible to you. There are many ways that you can stay in touch with a distant grandchild. You can continue to build a soulful relationship with a grandchild who is far away, as long as you are not prohibited by some legal action from having contact with him. Even if you have been through litigation and have been prohibited from having contact with your grandchild, situations can always change. There are many organizations that can help you to learn more about your rights as a grandparent. Contact the Legal Counsel for the Elderly through your local Area Agency on Aging or the American Civil Liberties Union for information and referrals.

Psychiatrist Arthur Kornhaber, in his book *Grandparent Power*, has recommended several strategies for establishing and maintaining intimate contact with grandchildren who live far away. You may want to try several approaches.

TIPS FOR BUILDING INTIMATE CONNECTIONS WITH DISTANT GRANDCHILDREN
(adapted from Kornhaber, 1994.)

Call often, but first check with parents and let them know your plans to be a frequent caller. Some grandparents in the Connecting the Generations focus groups told us that they have given phone cards to their grandchildren so they can feel free to call as well.
Treat yourself to a VCR and send your grandchild tapes of yourself telling stories, sharing anecdotes about your family, and doing things that your grandchild enjoys doing with you.
Exchange audiotapes – your grandchild's gurgles and coos in exchange for your "I love you."
If you can afford it, give your grandchild her own fax machine for a birthday or holiday and ask her to send you art work and special messages. Keep the faxes moving in her direction as well.
Use your computer. Even very young children can learn to respond to pictures and sounds sent via e-mail. If you have the right computer, modem, and software you can chat with your grandchild in real time. A camera mounted over your monitor can send pictures as you chat. New hardware and software are being introduced so rapidly that more "magic" will be possible by the time this book is printed. Some grandparents have home pages on the Internet for themselves and their grandchildren. Have fun!
Write good old-fashioned letters. Draw pictures, send a stick of gum, stickers, or a gift certificate for a hamburger or pizza. Small gifts can be loads of fun for kids.
Send photos. By the middle of his second year, around 15-18 months, your grandchild can learn to recognize your picture. Ask his parents to show it to him as you talk on the phone. Your local copy store may have a scanning service so you can scan your pictures onto a disk and send them via the Internet.

For others of you, the problem is not separation. On the contrary, your grandchildren are in your homes or you are in theirs because you are providing full time care in place of their parents. You are among the nearly 4 million families in which grandparents and grandchildren live together and the 1-1/2 million grandparents who are primarily responsible for your grandchild's care. Your generation has filled the parenting gap left by young people whose lives are out of control. Teens and young adults in our society face terrible problems such as chemical abuse, crime, gang violence, mental illness, and HIV/AIDS infection. Some physicians who treat stress-related ailments among grandparent caregivers have told me that we have lost much of our society's generation of young parents and we need to focus our social programming on their children – your grandchildren – who can still be saved. That is a harsh perspective born in the trenches of modern family life. Some of you have felt the pain of turning helplessly away from your child in order to rescue your dear grandchild from a dysfunctional home.

For others of you, the problems are different. Your grandchild needs your help to understand the losses that come with divorce, a parent's death, or the temporary breakup of his home. What do you tell a child who is crying because he must move out of his house, leave his friends, and adjust to losing mom or dad from his everyday family? You may find yourself trying to explain to your grandchild something that you do not yourself understand. You did the best you could in raising your children. You wanted them to have happy family lives and to find love that would last forever. How did this happen? How did *your* daughter find herself getting a divorce and bringing her child back home to live with you? Why did *your* son have to die in a senseless car accident? In his book *When Bad Things Happen to Good People*, Harold Kushner reminds us that as human beings, we are "free to hurt each other." Perhaps you will never understand why good people die or why good marriages go wrong, but you can help your grandchild to know that someone who loves her is always there. You can be the connection that links your grandchild to your religion or other sustaining belief system. You can show him that other people in his family and community are ready to help him make it through the difficult times. Connections – raising a grandchild is about building connections.

What are the big payoffs for all this effort at establishing and maintaining close relationships with grandchildren? You probably have thought of these rewards on your own, but let's look at them together.

- You are privileged to have the confidence and love of that dear person who is your grandchild.
- You establish relationships that will continue throughout your life – perhaps into a time when you are frail and need assistance from your family.
- You learn your own capacity to love.

Whenever you offer your strength to sustain your grandchild in a time of despair, whenever you close around your grandchild the protective blanket of family love, your heart is touched and your soul grows. I once had a colleague who signed all his letters, business or personal, "In the Dance." I asked him why and he told me that all people are in the dance of life together. We hold hands during times of joy or sorrow, futility or productivity, the comings and goings of life...and we move as one to the rhythm of life's music as it plays on...and on...and on.

WEEK ONE

WHAT MY GRANDPARENTS MEANT TO ME

What do you remember of your own grandparents? How did they connect with you? Can you describe them physically? Do you remember any "secrets" that they told you or any that you told them? In the space provided, write about your relationship with your grandparents. Thinking about the past may give you ideas to use right now in connecting with your grandchild.

_____

_____

_____

_____

_____

_____

_____

_____

_____

_____

_____

_____

_____

_____

_____

_____

_____

_____

_____

_____

_____

_____

WEEK TWO

MY FRIENDSHIP PYRAMID

Adult friendships can be described as a pyramid. At the top of the pyramid are you and your "best" friends. If you are married, you may have "couple friends." You may think of your spouse as a friend as well. Many people have friends who are also family members. If you work or belong to clubs, you may have friends among your contacts in those organizations. Chances are good that your closest friends were once somewhere else on the pyramid. Think about your friendships. Fill in the blanks that represent your many levels of friends. Put your "best" friends at the top of the pyramid and move out so that your casual friends and acquaintances are farthest from you. Use first names only.

Look at all the friendships that support you. WOW! Is the list longer than you expected? If you knew that everyone was about to turn to sand and you would have only one friend left, who would you want that person to be? Remember, we all need at least one essential person, a confidante, in order to be healthy and happy. You are fortunate if you have many friends and many supportive relationships.

ME

_____
(My best friend)

_____

_____

_____

_____

WEEK THREE

ADMISSION TO THE SECRET GARDEN

The relationship that you build with your very young grandchild will be the basis for later feelings of confidence, trust, and sharing. Children and adolescents are not very tolerant of adults who "fake it." If you want your grandchild to accept you in his confidence, you must earn your place there. One of my favorite stories is *The Secret Garden* because it captures that wonderful ability that children have to transport themselves back and forth from fantasy to reality while learning from each realm. Being in the confidence of your grandchild means that sometimes you may have to believe – really believe – that a sheet draped between two of your dining room chairs is an ancient fortress that must be defended. If you want your grandchild to follow you into the adult world of trust and caring, then you must begin by following her to Sesame Street or down the Yellow Brick Road or through the Strawberry Fields. Here are some tips that may help to put you and your grandchild at the same starting place. If you are genuinely interested in your grandchild's world, then he may accept you there and he may become more interested in your world as well.

TIPS FOR GAINING ADMISSION TO A CHILD'S SECRET GARDEN
Keep in touch with your grandchild's popular culture. Keep learning as your grandchild moves through developmental stages. Watch his Saturday morning cartoons. Walk through the toy department at a retail store. Go into an "alternative" music shop. Add to your car radio's auto select buttons a setting for a "Top Ten" station. Surf the Internet under "Kids" or "Teens" and see for yourself what is interesting to your grandchild.
Never use "kid language" if you do not know what you are saying. Listen to real kids and try to learn what they mean by terms you don't understand. Then keep quiet! It is better to listen knowingly than to irritate your grandchild by using her language with an adult twist.
Allow your grandchild to suggest activities that you can do together. Follow him into his secret garden – don't break down the gate.
Never betray your grandchild's confidence. Do not read diaries or other private communications. Do not "rat" on your grandchild to her parents. If she tells you something that parents need to know, encourage her to tell them. Offer to go with her if that makes her feel supported, but do not tell the "secret" unless keeping it presents threats to life or health.

Use this space to write for yourself three principles for confidential behavior between you and your grandchild. For example, "I will not promise to keep a secret unless I know I can keep the promise."

Never violate your own principles in relating to your grandchild as a confidante.

Principle #1 _____

Principle #2 _____

Principle #3 _____

WEEK FOUR

JUST BETWEEN "US"

Now it is time to start something really fun with your grandchild. If you want to be a friend and confidante, you must share some safe and healthy secrets. One of the best ways is to create something together that is totally your own. If your grandchild is an infant, you will have to wait a couple of years for this activity, but you can start to plan now. You will be surprised how soon you and your grandchild can start creating together.

Invest in two audio tape recorders, one for you and one for your grandchild, and some blank tapes. Be certain that both use the same size tapes. Some toy manufacturers make recorders with large control buttons. Your grandchild may be able to use one of these before he could manage an adult recorder. Decide on an introduction for a running tale that you and your grandchild will write together. Write the introduction here. Tape the introduction and give it to your grandchild. Ask him to "compose" the next section, tape it, and give the tape back to you. Keep the flow going back and forth. It is a good idea to throw in a "cliff-hanger" every now and then in order to grab your grandchild's attention. You will love the creative results!

Start your story...

Quite a long time ago _____

_____

_____

_____

_____

_____

_____

_____

_____

_____

_____

_____

_____

_____

_____

_____

_____

_____

_____

_____

_____

_____

_____

_____

You can prepare your infant grandchild for this activity by reading to her and telling her stories. Try making up tales using names and places that are familiar to her. Bring her into the process of the story. Ask questions and allow her to supply names or sounds. Later, she can make up new endings to the stories or drop in names and places, or together you can draw or paint simple illustrations. Pretty soon, you will be ready to create your own tale.

From these early shared experiences, your grandchild will learn that connecting with you is fun and safe. The constant, steady, positive reminder that you are there is powerful glue for holding the relationship that you want to have with your grandchild.

REFLECTIONS ON OUR STORY

When I told the story, my grandchild...

_____

_____

_____

_____

_____

_____

_____

_____

_____

_____

_____

_____

_____

_____

_____

_____

_____

_____

_____

_____

_____

_____

_____

_____

_____

_____

_____

_____

_____

_____

CHAPTER 11

KEEPING UP APPEARANCES:

GOOD MANNERS AND KIND BEHAVIOR

Let me assure you that you and your grandchild have at least one thing in common. Each of you hopes that the other will make it through most of life's little occasions without bringing humiliation on the family. I once saw a cartoon of what I believe is every adolescent's dream parent. There was no caption under this cartoon, simply a woman standing with a drink in her hand. She was wearing a dress that was exactly the same pattern as the wallpaper behind her. Do you remember wishing that your parents would just fade into the background? Later in your life, do you remember hoping that no one at the family picnic would notice the third ring in your daughter's ear or your son's new tattoo? It seems that much of the time, good manners are more a matter of avoiding social disasters than accomplishing much in the realm of social interaction.

When our focus group grandparents told us that teaching their grandchildren manners and proper behavior was a high priority, I was somewhat surprised. I thought that etiquette for most families today was something you: (a) misspelled in a crossword puzzle, (b) paid $21.95 for a book on the subject a month before your daughter's wedding, or (c) worried about only when addressing college graduation invitations to divorced friends. To think that grandparents were still, in 1997, worried about how their grandchildren behave in public was both refreshing and disquieting.

I wondered why grandparents were concerned about manners. Why did they feel that they would be the ones who had major responsibility to teach their grandchildren society's rules and family's order? The Southern Belle in my soul said, "I'll think about that tomorrow." But the sociologist in me said, "Instruction in etiquette must fulfill some latent need of grandparents to maintain control over family rules." You will be glad to know that the human being in me triumphed and I am writing this chapter from neither of the aforementioned perspectives. I have decided that Letitia Baldrige and Judith Martin (Miss Manners) are correct in their separate but similar assessments which affirm that manners are of interest to anyone concerned about children because there are people in our society who are: "sick of rudeness, aggression, and unruly behavior" and "worried about the future of civilization."

The ideology of the new etiquette is that we need to teach our children kind behavior based on respect and compassion for others. That sounds pretty simple. Most of the world's major religions have some directive to treat others as you want to be treated. But the notion of putting kindness into everyday life is not as widely practiced as it is prescribed. Listen to a popular comedian doing a routine on marriage. Chances are that most of the jokes you find funny are based on derisive comments of spouses about each other. Go to a children's baseball or soccer game and listen to the young players and parents as well rail the coaches and curse the umpires. Where is my competitive spirit? My only concern is that the hostility and aggression with which we laugh and play may find their way into the treatment of husbands and wives, parents and children, teachers and students, until kindness is lost and civility is only a part of our gentler past.

I am delighted to see that the new etiquette books for children address the values that are the basis for civil behavior, rather than superficially presenting the rules of "proper" behavior. If you are serious about being your grandchild's instructor and mentor in manners, I suggest that you investigate these excellent resources:

- Baldrige, Letitia (1997). *More Than Manners! Raising Today's Kids to Have Kind Manners and Good Hearts*. New York: Rawson Associates.

- Martin, Judith (1984). *Miss Manners' Guide to Rearing Perfect Children*. New York: Atheneum.

- Bates, Karen Grigsby & Hudson, Karen Elyse (1996). *Basic Black: Home Training for Modern Times*. New York: Doubleday.

You and I learned about manners in a different time. The rules were important, but no one told us the reasons. I can remember pouring over pictures of silver flatware. My mother liked to place the dessert fork on the outside of her place setting because it was smaller than the dinner fork. She thought that the symmetry of the setting was better when larger items were placed closer to the plate. Never mind that her guests might be rule-mongers as was I at age 9. Why, they might have well-founded expectations of moving from the outside of the place setting toward their plates as they consumed the various courses of the dinner. I remember arming myself with table diagrams from the gurus of grace in my time, Emily Post and Gloria Vanderbilt, and "winning" the argument over dessert fork placement. What I did not realize was that my mother understood that etiquette was not always about following the rules. For her, the point of a formal dinner was for a host to welcome guests into the warmth and creativity of her home, and to do so with her own charm and style. Now, I get it, Mom.

Children feel comfortable with rules. You can begin to teach a child about etiquette as soon as he is ready for social relationships. Whenever a child can respond to "no-no" by pulling away her hand, she is showing you that she has some degree of self-control. Sometime around his tenth month, your grandchild will show an interest in people. He can say "bye-bye" and wave hello and goodbye. These are simple social greetings, but they can be early building blocks of kind and considerate behavior. Did you ever have the experience of having an adult walk into your house and head directly for your TV set to turn on the football game that he was missing during the drive over? That kind of behavior brings out the worst in me. I mean, I start to have visions of myself serving the bean dip from his shirt pocket. Maybe his grandmother never told him that saying "hello" is a good thing and makes the host feel appreciated.

You can make progress with instruction in etiquette while your grandchild is a preschooler, but older children are better able to be flexible; that is, to accept situational changes in the rules. Your expectations about success in manners instruction should be linked closely with what is developmentally appropriate for the child's stage of moral development. Since moral development has to do with rules and conventions about the behavior of people toward each other, what is developmentally appropriate to teach a child about moral behavior may also apply to her "proper" social behavior. Your grandchild must be able to reason or think about rules, to behave according to rules or principles, and to have some feelings about following or breaking rules or resisting temptation before you can expect to see much in regard to either ethical behavior or value driven manners.

This table shows some of the milestones of moral development of a child, as described in the research of psychologist Lawrence Kohlberg. You may use them as reference points for developing your expectations about when your grandchild may be able to understand why good manners, fair treatment, and caring are important in our relationships. As with any developmental scheme, the Kohlberg stages should be only a guide. Your grandchild is an individual who will develop at her own pace. Watch for signals and be ready to help guide her toward being the kind and caring person that she has the potential for being.

KOHLBERG'S LEVELS OF MORAL DEVELOPMENT
Preconventional morality (before age 9): • Children obey because adults tell them to obey; goal is to avoid punishment. • Children obey what they want to obey; do what feels good, and what is rewarding.
Conventional morality (by early adolescence): • Children value trust, caring, and loyalty; seek to gain approval and to be thought of by family members as "good". • Moral judgments are based on conformity to society's rules.
Postconventional morality (never achieved by the majority of people): • Morality is completely internalized and based on principles and a personal moral code.

Another psychologist, Carol Gilligan, has suggested that Kohlberg's levels by far underemphasize the sense of caring that motivates many people. We know from research on early childhood that children as young as two or under show altruistic behaviors that appear to be appropriate demonstrations of sympathy and guilt feelings. This is particularly true of children who have had early group experiences such as day care or play groups. Watch your young grandchild's behavior when she sees another child crying. She may go to him and hug or pat him or say "There, there." She is demonstrating her sense of care.

Later, as adults, we respond to the needs of others out of motivations to care. There are situations when caring is almost illogical, but the need to care is strong. John Kingery was abandoned by his daughter at an Idaho race track. Security people found him sitting in a wheel chair with a box of adult diapers in his lap and a sign that said, "John King." His picture on national TV became the symbol of "granny dumping," the problem of elder abandonment by exhausted, financially burdened, and burned out caregivers. A granddaughter saw Mr. Kingery on the nightly news and told her grandmother, "I think this is Granddad." Nancy, another of Mr. Kingery's daughters, had been estranged from her father since shortly after her parents' divorce some 30 years earlier. She told me in an interview, "When I saw that it was my dad, I knew I had to go get him and take care of him. It was just something in my gut. It was something I had to do." Humans respond to each other from a need to care. Gilligan and others have reminded us that those feelings of care exist even when we are very young. You can foster those feelings in your grandchildren – boys and girls. Someday, you may benefit as Mr. Kingery did from having family members whose first reaction to your need is to provide for your care.

Some child development experts find Kohlberg's scheme of moral development not only lacking in the dimension of care but also in its precision in explaining the "morality" of young children. Psychologists J. L. Carroll and J. R. Rest in their discussion of the moral development of children have suggested that it is more helpful to think of moral behavior than stages of moral developmental. You can use their four components of moral behavior as a measure of your grandchild's development as a caring and kind person. These four steps in behaving morally are:

- Moral sensitivity – recognizing a moral problem;
- Moral judgment – deciding what is right or wrong by critical thinking;
- Moral values – having ideals, values, or what we call "a conscience"; and
- Moral action – behaving in an ethical way.

Whatever scheme you use to think about your grandchild's moral behavior, remember that he must be guided by example and tried by experience if he is to become a kind and caring person who treats others ethically. Your example and the example of his parents and other adults in his family environment will have the strongest lasting effect of any influence on his character. Research with adolescents and young adults has shown that family influence is in the end the most important determinant of a person's moral behavior.

If your grandchild is a preschooler or younger, you may find that the work of psychologist Jean Piaget is more useful than Kohlberg's in helping you to understand the child's moral development. This table shows the developmental stages of moral behavior in children twelve and under. Note that Piaget's scheme breaks down the younger ages to give you a better idea of what may be happening while your grandchild is an infant or toddler, a preschooler, and a grade school or middle school child.

PIAGET'S SEQUENCE OF MORAL DEVELOPMENT IN CHILDREN (ages 0-12)
Ages 0-3 – There are no rules recognized by the child. He does what he wants. Limitations are from outside.
Ages 3-7 – The child imitates rule-following behavior. She can be influenced by others' behavior or suggestions. She will not follow rules if she does not want to. She may want to enforce rules for your behavior, but not for her own.
Ages 7-10 – The child understands manners and will play by mutually accepted rules.
Ages 10-12 – Rules exist to make the game possible. Rules can be suspended or changed, but only by mutual agreement.

An important aspect of kind and courteous behavior is the use of language to express feelings. Right now, you get excited about any verbalization that you hear from your grandchild – sounds, syllables, words, or phrases – but eventually, you will want him to be your conversational partner. As his language skills increase, you can steer him into polite and interesting exchanges. Here are some suggestions for conversation development from linguistics expert Dr. Naomi Baron. You may find them helpful in building your grandchild's skills in talking with others.

- Use an interactive rather than directive conversational style when talking to your grandchild.
- Remember to listen – allow your grandchild to talk and do not interrupt his sentences.
- Be aware of your own pronunciations, meanings, and conversational formats.
- Reinforce and expand the child's development in sound, meaning, and conversation.
- Ask for clarification when you do not understand what your grandchild is saying.

Once your grandchild is developmentally ready to be a conversational partner, the fun really gets underway! Don't you just love to swap stories of "cute" or "smart" things your grandchild has said? Why, that can be as much fun as showing pictures. Now comes the time for teaching your grandchild that language as well as action needs to be appropriate for the situation and motivated by kindness and consideration for those around her. There are many venues through which your grandchild may use his newly acquired conversational skills. Besides face-to-face conversation, your grandchild needs to learn how to be courteous in using the telephone, e-mail, and written letters. You can be a model by using all of these methods of communication to stay in contact with your grandchild. Be sure that she learns that letters and phone calls are appropriate to use to express feelings.

Abby, aged three, was sitting at the kitchen table when her grandfather got a phone call. She overheard him using the name Lucy for his caller. The caller was an 80-year-old friend of the family who was checking the time and date of an upcoming party, but Abby knew only that her name was Lucy. Abby had a friend at preschool whose sister Lucy had recently lost a tooth. Abby tugged on her grandfather's shirt sleeve. "I want to talk to Lucy," she asked. At first, he ignored the tugs, but then decided that it might be fun to hear what his granddaughter would say to an 80-year-old woman. He gave the phone to Abby who consolingly said, "Lucy, I'm sorry you lost your tooth," and handed the phone back to her grandfather. Lucy's roaring laughter was enough to make her reaction clear. Abby had made a courteous and supportive gesture, although misdirected. Children need to learn to make friendship calls as well as to accurately relay telephone messages and to use the phone for safety.

Kind and gentle behaviors need to be modeled in the relationships which the child observes every day. Good manners begin in the family environment. Your grandchild needs to see the following from you and other adults in the family:

- Kind and courteous treatment between spouses;
- Consideration of the feelings of children;
- Respect and kindness toward older people;
- Respect for authority;
- Reverence for the sacred or spiritual symbols that are important to your family;
- Respect for the dignity of all people; and
- Care for animals and the environment in which we live.

As you work through the exercises in this chapter, remember that caring connects. Think about how you can help your grandchild to care for the people, animals, and things around him, and you will be near your goal of having a well-mannered, kind, and good-hearted grandchild.

WEEK ONE

AGES & STAGES

Read the following scenarios and, using the information from Piaget and Kohlberg on stages of moral development, decide for each: (1) the child's age, (2) the child's reasoning process, and (3) the appropriate response that the grandparent should make.

Scenario #1 – "The Board Game"

Lou and her grandson Terry were playing a board game. Each player was to roll the dice and move the indicated number of places on the board. Lou rolled a 3. Disappointedly, she said, "Oh, I wanted a 5 so I could move to the red space." Terry picked up the dice and turned them until 5 dots were visible. "There Grannylou," he announced,"Now you can move to the red space."

Approximately how old is Terry? _____

What did Terry think that made him decide to behave as described?_____

_____

_____

_____

_____

_____

_____

What would you do if you were "Grannylou"? _____

_____

_____

_____

_____

_____

_____

Scenario #2 – "Out to Lunch"

Carol invited her daughter Cindy and granddaughter Beth out for lunch at a small cafe. When Cindy and Beth arrived, Carol noticed that Beth was wearing blue jeans under her sun dress. Beth refused the booster chair that the server offered and spent most of the meal under the table. About halfway through the meal, Beth emerged from underneath the table and began making rounds of the other tables in the restaurant. At some tables, she stopped and smiled sweetly. Whenever she saw a tip left on a table, she took the money and stuffed it in her jeans pocket.

Approximately how old is Beth? _____

What did Beth think that made her decide to behave as described? _____

_____

_____

_____

_____

_____

_____

What would you do if you were Carol? _____

_____

_____

_____

_____

_____

_____

Scenario #3 – "This Is Not a Bus"

Eric and Samantha were playing on Eric's basement stairs. Small empty cardboard boxes lined the stairs, two to a step. A book was placed beside each box. Eric sat on the bottom step with a book in his lap. Samantha stood in front of the pretend classroom and delivered a lecture on how to make the rain fall. Suddenly, Eric screamed at Samantha, "Get out of the way or this bus will run over you." Samantha screamed back and started to cry, "This is not a bus. This is school, you dummy!" Eric ran up the stairs and called for his mom. "Samantha can't play here anymore," he sobbed.

Approximately how old are Eric and Samantha? _____

What did Eric and Samantha think that made them decide to behave as described? _____

_____

_____

_____

_____

_____

What would you do if you were Eric's mom? _____

_____

_____

_____

_____

_____

_____

Scenario #4 – Write your own...

Use this space to write a situation which you have handled with your grandchild. Think about your response and its consequences. Would you handle the situation the same way if it happened today?

_____

_____

_____

_____

_____

_____

_____

Approximately how old was your grandchild when this happened? _____

What did he or she think that made him or her decide to behave as described?

_____

_____

_____

_____

_____

_____

What would you do if you could replay the scene? _____

_____

_____

_____

_____

_____

_____

WEEK TWO

GRAN'S TOP TEN LIST

Comedian David Letterman has brought the "Top Ten List" into our popular culture. There is now a site on the Internet where you can read Letterman's Top Ten List on a variety of topics. Copycat Top Ten Lists are everywhere. Create your own "Top Ten Most Embarrassing Things My Grandchild Could Do In Public." Start with #10, the least embarrassing, and move toward #1, the most embarrassing. Decide how you could prevent each embarrassing situation by helping your grandchild to develop good manners before they happen.

#10 _____

#9 _____

#8 _____

#7 _____

#6 _____

#5 _____

#4 _____

#3 _____

#2 _____

#1 _____

WEEK THREE

MORAL PRINCIPLES

Your grandchild will develop good manners and ethical behavior mostly by watching you and his parents. This is a good time to think about the principles that guide your behavior. Use this page to record what you believe are the most important principles of good manners and ethical behavior in your own life. These are your essentials.

Principles of Good Manners for Me

_____

_____

_____

_____

Principles of Ethical Behavior for Me

_____

_____

_____

_____

What principles do you want to instill in your grandchild? Are they the same as the principles that have guided you? Are there new principles that you think will be important to your grandchild but were not so important to you? Has your daughter-in-law or son-in-law brought new guiding principles into your family?

Principles of Good Manners for My Grandchild

_____

_____

_____

_____

Principles of Ethical Behavior For My Grandchild

_____

_____

_____

_____

WEEK FOUR

THE MANNERS GAME

From the first time you smiled and said, "What a good girl!" to reward your granddaughter's wave bye-bye, you have been teaching her to be considerate in a world that may not be considerate to her. You are careful to create a safe environment for her to practice her good manners. You also make sure that each thoughtful act she does is rewarded with attention and praise. Sometimes you teach manners by making a game in which your grandchild practices following rules, taking turns, and praising others.

What is your favorite game to play with your grandchild? _____

_____

_____

What are the rules of good behavior in this game? _____

_____

_____

What are the consequences for breaking the rules of this game? _____

_____

_____

What are the rewards for good behavior while playing this game? _____

_____

_____

What principles of good manners and ethical behavior are taught in this game?

_____

_____

_____

Write your reflections on the first time you saw your grandchild show good manners or helpful behavior. _____

_____

_____

_____

_____

_____

_____

_____

_____

_____

_____

Remember, the best way to teach your grandchild to have good manners and a kind and gentle spirit is to model those traits in your own life. Your thoughtfulness and consideration will teach your grandchild to treat others with honor and respect.

CHAPTER 12

CLOSING THE CIRCLE:
CONNECTING THE GENERATIONS THROUGH STORIES, MYTHS, AND SONGS

*"You can keep an old tradition going only
by renewing it in terms of a current circumstance."*

– Joseph Campbell

The stories we tell our children and grandchildren are powerful conveyors of the rules for today and our collective memories of yesterday. Think about the story of Little Red Riding Hood. The images presented are of vulnerable females, elderly people who are both frail and nurturing, dangerous possibilities lurking in the persons of strangers or the uncertainty of places unknown, and ultimate rescue by a gallant champion. Such stories draw on our individual fears and hopes for the future. At the same time they remind our children of our collective values. Among those values are that home and family are the safest places and that even the most formidable enemy can be defeated with a little help from a kind-hearted soul who has a sense of fairness and right.

Humans involve their infants in the myths of their societies even before the children are born. Myths explaining the mystery of conception and childbirth reflect family structures, roles, and beliefs. These examples of conception myths have been discussed by anthropologist Dr. Lynn Morgan. In the matrilineal society of the Ashanti of West Africa, inheritance and naming follow the mother's family line. The Ashanti believe that the body of the baby is formed from the mother's blood. The father makes no contribution to the child's physical being. Instead, he contributes the baby's soul and in so doing begins a lifelong spiritual connection with his child. Traditional conception myths in Malaysia, a patrilineal society where inheritance and naming follow the male bloodline, are quite different. The child is thought to begin in the father's brain and to drift down his body until it is finally deposited in the mother's womb for development. As these and other myths of conception are passed from generation to generation, so are traditional beliefs about the relative roles of men and women and the structure of families in societies.

Once a child is born, we begin to engage him in the myths of our society from very early on. Lullabies are the baby's introduction into a society's mythology. By the way, it is not always the mother who sings these lullabies. Fathers and grandparents are often the singers, while mothers maintain stronger roles as disciplinarians. Dr. Kris Hardin, University of Pennsylvania anthropology professor, helped organize an extensive look at the relationships of adults to children in various societies. The Smithsonian Institution exhibition was called Generations and opened in 1987. Dr. Hardin identified four major types of lullabies: sleep inducing rhythms and soothing sounds; reminders of the dearness and value of children; promises of good things, usually in exchange for falling asleep; and threats of bad things if the baby does not fall asleep. Are you singing to your grandchildren the songs that your parents or grandparents sang to you? Are your family beliefs evident in those songs? Will the songs that you sing to your grandchild have any influence on her beliefs? Here is the lullaby that generations of children in my family have heard. If you get past the nearly nonsensical words, the message is one of healthy inquiry into principles of science and nature, the kindness of a powerful spiritual figure who is touched by creature's needs, and the value of communication. Hmm, I wonder if it is coincidental that our family has within three generations who have been rocked to sleep to this song, three ministers, seven Ph.D. and master's degrees, four school teachers, three therapists, several musicians and writers, and a budding environmental scientist.

Baby bye, here's a fly;
We will watch it, you and I;
How it crawls, up the walls,
Yet it never falls.

Tongues to talk have you and I.
God has given a little fly
No such things,
So he sings
With his buzzing wings.

Stories, myths, and songs draw us into a shared experience. A grandmother who grew up in a rural area, rarely leaving the farm, can share with her grandson in the big city the experiences of Johnny Appleseed or Hansel and Gretel. Together a 60-year-old grandparent and a 4-year-old grandchild can climb on board behind "The Little Engine That Could"and travel past the years that separate their ages. Tangible connections are built by grandparents repeating stories, reading the same books over and over, and memorizing songs together with their grandchildren.

These shared experiences define the family circle. They draw the child inside who you are as a family. "When a magician wants to work magic, he puts a circle around himself and it is within this bounded circle, this hermetically sealed-off area, that powers can be brought into play that are lost outside the circle," Joseph Campbell, renowned mythologist, reminds us. You will see your special powers whenever you put a blanket on the grass and say to your grandchild, "Let's sit on this magic carpet while we read a story." You will know the magic is there when your grandchild climbs into the circle of your arms and asks, "Read me a story, Gran."

The easiest way for you to get started telling stories to your grandchild is to read to him. When you read a book to your grandchild, you are borrowing someone else's story, but you are making your own experience. Most children's books have illustrations that the child will enjoy. You can engage your grandchild in the story by asking her to tell you about the pictures or to point to objects in the illustrations. I remember a visit from my sister when my children were very young. She is a great storyteller and reader. My son had a favorite story about a cat who was a detective. It was a rather long and descriptive story which he enjoyed hearing at bedtime. My usual "tired mom" method of reading was to follow the story line but to turn 2-3 pages at a time in order to cut a half-hour story to about 10 minutes. Well, Ms. Folklore, otherwise known as my sister, not only read the entire story, but used different voices for each character and then reread the story so my son could create a new ending. After her week-long visit, bedtime story telling was never the same. Of course over 20 years later, my son and my sister have a marvelous relationship. He now enjoys reading stories to her grandchildren. Oh yes, he is also a professional writer. You never know what may come of a connection. Connections – story telling, reading, singing lullabies, bringing a child into your magic circle – it's all about connections.

Did I mention that your grandchild is a wonderful one-person audience? If you never had that lead in your high school play or that call from Broadway, you can be a star in your grandchild's eyes. If you decide to sharpen your storytelling skills, there are some good resource books and help on the Internet. I found a wonderful website on "Telling Family Stories" by Miriam H. Nade (http://www.cinenet.net/users/mhnadel/story/family.html). She defines a family story as any incident that is told about a family member over several years. Such stories involve a crisis, not necessarily a negative event, and its resolution. There is some learning from the story, and usually a recounting of how the crisis and its resolution changed the main character or the family. Sometimes family stories are simply several linked anecdotes about a person or a family. Ms. Nadel suggests these possible family story lines:

- the story behind your last name;
- the place you grew up;
- a family celebration, ritual, or tradition;
- family vacations,
- how parents or grandparents met;
- a secret hiding place that you had as a child;
- what the family did when someone got ill.

When you tell your story, Ms. Nadel suggests using gestures, different voices for the characters, and postures that illustrate what is happening or bring you and the child together in different ways. Your story needs to be based on true happenings, but it does not need to follow every boring detail. You can tell a true story that has been modified so it is more interesting to the child.

One grandfather that I know said that he started to keep a journal when he became a grandfather because he wanted to be the person who told his own story. There is something rather powerful about writing, or telling, your personal and family history. You maintain control over the knowledge your grandchild has about your family. You can interpret family events any way you like. You can convey impressions about family members. In effect, you become the family historian.

One word of caution before we leave our discussion of family stories and myths. Family myths can produce negative consequences if they prevent people in the family from obtaining and using information that would help them or strengthen the family. One example of the use of negative family myths is the creation of family stories that hide family secrets and prevent family members from talking out their real problems. Another example is in the area of health care.

I have been working with some colleagues in the College of Medicine at the university where I teach to examine the effects of second-time parenting on grandmothers who have arthritis. Our findings are very similar to those of Dr. Meredith Minkler and her colleagues at the University of California, School of Public Health, Berkeley. Grandmothers who are primary caregivers for their grandchildren are stoic about their own health problems. Indeed, they may neglect treatment for their own health problems in order to continue to care for their grandchildren. One reason for this self-neglect is scarce family resources, including lack of money or insurance for health care and lack of back-up caregivers if they need hospitalization. But another reason seems to be related to family myths about health care and about "getting old." Many of the grandmothers who come into the clinics where my colleagues practice report that they believe that arthritis is just something you expect to have when you get older. The family stories that they have heard depict older people as "crippled" or "stove up." Children in these families are taught through the family stories that it is normal for older people to have pain as part of the natural aging process. Further, since many older people die in nursing homes or hospitals, family stories have been woven around the myth that you fare much better if you can stay out of the formal health care system as long as possible. These women have also been told in the myths of their families that women are supposed to take care of anyone in the family who needs them. Often, they see themselves as the glue that holds the family together. They do fulfill an essential role in their families, but it is unfortunate when they allow their self-image as caregiver to prevent them from seeking medical attention that could make them feel better now and prevent worse health problems in the future.

The point is to avoid creating or perpetuating family myths that prevent family members from acting on accurate information or that discourage family members from confronting issues which can be dealt with and resolved. With care, you can use family myths to teach your grandchildren "how we do things" and still give them the freedom to be creative in finding solutions for new situations that earlier generations in the family have never had to face.

The exercises in this chapter will help you to examine the family stories and myths that you heard and to develop skills in using stories, myths, and songs with your grandchild. Have fun, be creative, and allow your grandchild to contribute. Good family stories are expandable. They incorporate the creative ideas of each person who gets involved with the telling. A family story can be a collection of connections between you and your history and you and the future generations of your family.

WEEK ONE

LULLABIES AND BIRTHDAYS

Special occasions often are accompanied by special songs or dances. Tomorrow, I plan to attend the Greek Festival in my community. There will be special foods and costumes. My favorite event every year is the dance that the old and young do together, in full traditional costume. It ends with everyone in a circle, dancing in perfect rhythm. I can almost feel the flow of family and community tradition.

When your family celebrates, do you sing or dance? What are your favorite family songs or dances? Write the words to songs that you remember. Include the lullaby that your parents or grandparents sang to you.

My Favorite Celebration Song

_____

_____

_____

_____

_____

_____

_____

My Favorite Lullaby

_____

_____

_____

_____

_____

_____

_____

My Favorite Patriotic Song or Song of Faith

_____

_____

_____

_____

_____

_____

My Favorite Silly Song

_____

_____

_____

_____

_____

_____

Teach your favorite songs to your grandchild. Don't worry if your musical talent is not the best. Your grandchild will love you for your efforts. Remember to tell your grandchild the stories that go along with these songs. Most of the fun is in bringing your grandchild in touch with your history.

WEEK TWO

A FAMILY ACTON STORY

Sometimes stories are acted out as well as being told. "Not me," you may be saying. "There is a reason for my not being on the stage. I'm a lousy actor!" Don't worry. Acting does not necessarily mean saying lines on a stage. I mean that you can put some action with your story. For example, the Kids' Storytelling Club is sponsoring a Family Diversity Storytelling Quilt as its current project. Each month, the Kids' Storytelling Club sponsors a new event related to storytelling with children. You can find the club at (http://www.storycraft.com/welcome.htm) on the Internet or you can write for any of their project ideas to:

> Bobbi Shupe
> P.O. Box 205
> Masonville, CO 80541-0205

Good ways to add action to your family stories are:

- Draw or paint a picture with your grandchild's help, or draw separate illustrations and compare.
- Make cookies or bread in the shape of some figure mentioned in the story, or make a favorite food mentioned in a holiday or celebration story.
- Cut pictures from a magazine and glue them onto poster board to make a family story collage.
- Look through family photo albums to find pictures of the people in the story.
- Show treasured mementoes or souvenirs from special occasions or family vacations in your stories.

Use this space to describe an activity that you and your grandchild have done or will do to accompany a family story. What was your grandchild's reaction? How do you feel about the experience? _____

_____

_____

_____

_____

_____

_____

WEEK THREE

FAIRY TALE FLAW FINDER

The quote from Joseph Campbell at the beginning of this chapter reminds us that traditions must be renewed. A corollary of that notion is that stories need to be updated from time to time in order to make them relevant for today's children. Some stories stand the test of time. Others do not. Sometimes children change stories to fit the world as they know it. In his book, *When Bad Things Happen to Good People*, Harold Kushner tells about a little boy who came home from Sunday School with a story to tell. His mother asked him what he had learned that morning and he said, "The Children of Israel were running from Pharaoh and they got to the Red Sea and could not get across. The Egyptian army was chasing them. They were scared so they got on their walkie talkies and called the Israeli army and they came and blew those Egyptians away. Then they built a bridge so the people could get across and everyone was safe again. The mother, a little surprised, asked, "Is that what they told you in Sunday School?" "No," the little boy replied, "But if I told you what they really told me, you'd never believe it."

Fairy tales have recently come under fire because of the traditional roles they assign to men and women and the violence that they portray. Use this exercise to examine whether your current values and beliefs are represented in the stories that you tell your grandchildren.

Choose your favorite fairy tale – one that you tell your grandchild. Read it or tell the story. As you move through the story, think about its message and the images that it presents. Write here:

(1) Messages that you would keep: _____

_____

_____

_____

_____

(2) Messages that you would like to change: _____

_____

_____

_____

WEEK FOUR

OUR FAMILY HISTORY

Here is your chance to write history. You may not have been there to record the chariot races in ancient Rome. You may have even missed capturing last year's Super Bowl game on your VCR. But you are here at this time, in this place, in this family! Use this space to write the outline of your family history. When you are ready, you can add details. You may want to start telling these stories to your grandchildren. You may also want to hear other versions of your family history from your parents, aunts and uncles, brothers and sisters, and your children.

People I Want to Remember

_____

_____

_____

Important Places

_____

_____

_____

Stories I Want to Keep from My Childhood

_____

_____

_____

Events That Are Important in Our Family

_____

_____

_____

Events That Are Important to Me

_____

_____

_____

Stories, myths, and songs can convey to your grandchild your family's history, your beliefs and values, and a sense of belonging. Include in your stories links to your grandchild's current world, and you will be able to keep traditions alive in your family. Be creative and open to your grandchild's new ideas, and you will be able to keep your family alive in your traditions.

Well, there it is. Thank you for spending this time with me.

You have taken the time to create a memory. As you and your grandchild continue your relationship, you will know that you have thought and planned and explored yourself in preparation for your marvelous journey. The grandparent that you will be comes from the you that you are. Soulful grandparenting starts with a knowledge and inner delight with your own being. How you make connections, what you believe, what you hope for the future, how you live – these are keys to the grandparent you will be. This book was designed to help you discover your wonderful living self and to take it into your relationship with your grandchild.

Of course, this book has been about your grandchild as well. That marvelous little person has already changed your life. You have looked at him and felt your heart slip into the clutches of his tiny hand. You have watched her run and jump into the safe circle of your arms and you have known that you will always be there for her. Your have felt the connection. Now, as you reflect on the exercises you just completed, you know that the connection will grow. Year after year, smile after smile, touch after touch, you and your grandchild will connect to each other.

What is even more wonderful is that in *Connecting the Generations* you will connect to the past and to the future of your family and you will connect to the world in which you live. Our world is a family of families. Connections – it's all about connections. One soul to another soul...to another time...to another life...on and on...life upon life.

Enjoy your grandchild and let her enjoy you. For the first time in our history, children will know healthy, active, participating grandparents well into their adulthood. Make the most of the opportunity that you have by being in this place at this time. Know that you are part of a growing alliance of grandparents who will positively influence lives in the new millennium.

All my best,

Roma

MORE TO READ ABOUT
GRANDPARENTS, CHILDREN, AND FAMILIES

Baldrige, Letitia, (1997). *More Than Manners! Raising Today's Kids to Have Kind Manners and Good Hearts.* New York: Rawson Associates.

Carson, L. (1996). *The Essential Grandparent.*
Deerfield Beach, FL: Health Communications, Inc.

Cherlin, A. & Furstenberg, F. (1986). *The New American Grandparent: A Place in the Family, A Life Apart.* New York: Basic Books.

Clinton, H.R. (1996). *It Takes a Village: And Other Lessons Children Teach Us.*
New York: Simon & Schuster.

Cohn, A. & Leach, L. (1987). *Generations: A Universal Family Album.*
New York: Pantheon Books.

Eyre, L. & Eyre, R. (1993). *Teaching Your Children Values.* New York: Fireside.

Kornhaber, A. (1994). *Grandparent Power!* New York: Crown Trade Paperbacks.

Kornhaber, A. (1996). *Contemporary Grandparenting.* Thousand Oaks, CA: Sage.

Minkler, M. & Roe, K. (1993). *Grandmothers as Caregivers: Raising Children of the Crack Cocaine Epidemic.* Newbury Park, CA: Sage.

Pipher, M. (1996). *The Shelter of Each Other: Rebuilding Our Families.*
New York: G.P. Putnam's Sons.

Prather, H. & Prather G. (1996). *Spiritual Parenting.*
New York: Three Rivers Press.

Takas, M. (1995). *Grandparents Raising Grandchildren: A Guide to Finding Help and Hope.* Brookdale Foundation Publication.

Westheimer, R., with Pierre A. Lehu. (1997). *Dr. Ruth Talks About Grandparents.*
New York: Farrar Straus Giroux.

Whalen, C.E. (1996). *The Featherbone Principle: A Declaration of Interdependence.*
Warren Featherbone Foundation Publication.

ABOUT THE AUTHOR

Dr. Roma Stovall Hanks has an M.A. in Clinical Psychology from George Peabody College of Vanderbilt University and a Ph.D. in Family Studies from the University of Delaware. She is currently Associate Professor of Sociology and Director of USA Programs in Gerontology at the University of South Alabama.

Dr. Hanks is former Chair of the Work and Family Focus Group of the National Council on Family Relations. She holds numerous professional memberships including the International Sociological Association, the American Sociological Association, and the Gerontological Society of America. She has received a number of honors including the 1990 Dissertation Award, Section on Aging, from the American Sociological Association and served as a member of the Editorial Board of Marriage and Family Review, a professional journal for research on families, published by Haworth Press. She has also served as project director for a grant provided for Interactive Planning for Family Futures, DHHS Administration on Aging.

Dr. Hanks has edited eight books in her general area of expertise, all published since 1990 by Haworth Press. In addition, she has written numerous book chapters and research articles, and presented at national and international conferences in the areas of family, aging, and inter-generational relationships.

Her current research focuses on grandparent care givers, spirituality, intimacy and health through the life course, and work/family issues.